WHAT gives?

by chelsea marie

Togi entertainment inc.
Subsidiary of The Owners Group Inc.

PUBLISHED BY

Togi Entertainment, Inc.
56 Expressway Place
5601 NW 72nd Street Suite 342
Oklahoma City, OK 73132
405-728-5536

Togi Entertainment, Inc.
602 South Broadway Avenue
Tyler, TX 75701
903-595-4249

Subsidiary of
The Owners Group, Inc.
Tyler, TX

PRINTED BY

AuthorHouse™
1663 Liberty Drive, Suite 200
Bloomington, IN 47403
www.authorhouse.com
Phone: 1-800-839-8640

AuthorHouse™ UK Ltd.
500 Avebury Boulevard
Central Milton Keynes, MK9 2BE
www.authorhouse.co.uk
Phone: 08001974150

First published by TogiEntertainment, Inc. 3/6/2007

ISBN: 978-1-4259-8545-5 (hc)
ISBN: 978-1-4259-8544-8 (sc)

Printed in the United States of America
Bloomington, Indiana

This book is printed on acid-free paper.

Warning: This book contains explicit language.

Every year, over 4,000 young people commit suicide. In 2002, there were over 132,000 suicide attempts in the United States, and suicide is the third leading cause of death among 15 to 24 year-olds. Although it's true that some of those children come from the stereotypical broken homes...homes characterized by extreme poverty, drug and alcohol abuse, and perhaps domestic violence or other childhood traumas, many of those troubled teenagers come from normal, middle class homes. Homes where the emotional cracks are small, where the sources of the inner turmoil are harder to pinpoint, and as a result, often go unrecognized. Homes that might be a lot like yours and mine.

Chelsea Marie's story is both universal and unique. What Gives? deals with subject matters that many might find controversial: family dynamics, depression, our mental health care system, drugs, alcohol, and, of course, suicide. It is unique because it is written in poetry form in "real time," which gives the reader an uneasy sense of actually seeing what Chelsea witnessed through her eyes, and of feeling what she experienced from the inside, as it happened. It is unique because, unlike most books written for and about teenagers, it is written from the perspective of...and by...an incredibly aware sixteen year-old. And finally, it is unique, and, in many ways, disturbing, because it was written as essentially a 350 page suicide note.

It is universal because it is, to one degree or another, almost every teenager's story. Although the details might vary from one individual to the next, every teenager will be able to relate to the inner struggle that Chelsea copes with, and, hopefully, they will learn from it. Parents might want to read it first, so that they can be better prepared to deal with the inevitable questions that could, and should, transpire between parent and teenager, and to be aware of the controversial and sensitive subject matters that What Gives? undertakes in a candid and honest way. The language is blunt and often harsh, written in the way that millions of teenagers speak to each other when they are hidden from the watchful eyes of their parents. Parents, teenagers, and young adults alike should read What Gives? so that they might gain a better understanding of what young people deal with every day, and recognize the warning signs...before it's too late.

About the Author:

Chelsea Marie is a sixteen year-old living in the Midwestern United States. She is an accomplished musician, artist, photographer, and writer. *What Gives?* is her first book.

Acknowledgements:
I would like to thank the following people for their help in making this book possible: Murray, Betty, Mr. Faulk (my second daddy), my family, the Academy, and the people who read it before I thought it was even good at all.   CM

www.TogiEntertainment.com
www.myspace.com/whatgives/

Subsidiary of The Owners Group Inc.

Entertainment for Heart, Mind, and Soul.

TogiEntertainment is a multi-media publishing and entertainment company that focuses on quality entertainment in all areas of publishing, movies, music, and broadcasting.

The publishers thank everyone at TogiEntertainment and The Owners Group Inc. for their dedication and efforts in making this book a reality, and our shareholders for believing in the dream.

www.TheOwnersGroupInc.com

Back cover photograph by Kelsey Renee.
All other photographs and artwork by Chelsea Marie.

for "the 7"
(especially my parents and my little brother)

...and for Betty

The first time I read Chelsea's book was the second time I met with her for therapy. I was aware she had been brought in for treatment due to suicidal thoughts, and we had started with the typical, "What brings you here?" and "How will I help?" Little did I know, Chelsea had her most private thoughts on paper, about 100 pages at the time, and was ready to share after knowing me for all of an hour.

The official assessment stated she had written a suicide note/plan, her parents and therapist had read it, and now she was sitting here with me. She offered to let me read her book, and I chuckled to myself when I saw how thick the stack of papers was and the fact it was in this tattered, blue folder. I could picture her carrying this with her everywhere. I told her, "I'm not sure if we will have time to go through all of this in the next hour, so I'll just take a quick look."

There was an Introduction section with several clever titles for her individual stories. I started scanning the headings, looking for the ones that would be relevant to our situation. I read the first page. I tried to stay neutral with my body language and my reaction, but quickly knew that would not happen. I believe my initial reaction was, "Wow," and I actually said this out loud.

Chelsea sat back on the couch, got comfortable, and I instantly knew she was different than any other adolescent I had talked to under these circumstances. She had a gift for storytelling, but this wasn't fiction. This was her life. A sixteen year-old girl, struggling with issues that anyone could identify with, yet able to communicate this to the reader as if they were reading their own life-story. This talented teenager had decided to retreat within herself when she feared others would not understand her. She was able to tell me what she was feeling, but had difficulty trusting those closest to her with how sad she was and how this had become her entire world.

This book is a chance for a quiet, shy girl to scream her message to anyone who can understand her. I think that's all of us.

While these stories are extremely personal for Chelsea and her family, I believe this can be a gift for so many other families struggling with a variety of issues. My experience as an adolescent and family therapist tells me this book can be an invaluable tool for helping members of a family improve their communication, their trust, and the joy that they give and receive with everyone they touch for the rest of their lives. I challenge any mother, father, brother or sister to read the first chapter and try not to read the rest. I couldn't, just like everyone else who has touched this book.

****

Murray Anderson is a Licensed Professional Counselor, who has worked in mental health since 1999. He specializes in working with adolescents and families, addressing such issues as depression, anger control, substance abuse and trauma. He is currently working in a children's/adolescent mental health hospital as well as seeing clients in private practice.

maybe
if i write a book

and i get real into it
and stuff

then i'll have to finish it.
and it will be the thing that keeps me alive.

because who wants to die with half
a fucking book written??

i don't want that for me.

i don't want that for anyone who ever reads a book.

so i think i'm going to try and finish this.

and i hope that it's a long one.
            i hope that it's a long one.

Part One

The Plan

part one

it's starting to seem like

mom and dad yell at me every night at dinner.

and it's starting to seem like

one day i will explode.

rosemary and i
out of an aluminum can we smoke

in the serenest of cemeteries
we share thoughts and laughs
and it is all twinkling.

rain splatters the windshield
of the warm car that envelops us
          in smoke
          in warmth
          in tittering giggles.

and i am looking down at my legs.

there are - GOSH - there are **so many holes** in my tights
that i have never never noticed before!!

as a kite

my eyeballs shrink
and my mouth goes dry

as rosemary drives us back to school
the trees are ten
thousand
times more beautiful

and i notice every detail.

the outlines of the houses jump
and then slowly the insides follow
when i turn my head
to look around.

i look to rosemary.
she is
sooooooo
funny she
is
sooooooo
great
God.
i love her.
i love her *so* much.

upon realizing this
i melt into my seat
and close my shrinking eyes.

my bones are so warm.

the night i knew i was starting to go crazy

i had just had a fight with my dad

and i was so so mad

that's when i went into my room

i turned off the lights

and i screamed

i screamed bloodcurdling screams

into the darkness of my room

and i held onto my head

my eyes were bulging

and the pressure from this ANGER

was turning my face bright red

and HOT

i rocked back and forth

faster and faster

and then i rolled around

falling off of my bed

hitting the floor with a THUD

the screams gave way to tears

lonely tears and sad tears and sorry tears

and oh-my-God-i'm-so-crazy tears.

it hasn't happened for a little while
but a week ago it
was still plaguing me

whenever i walked through a hallway
(it started at school)
or anywhere crowded
full of airsucking talking moving shoving pushing screaming people

i would feel as though
i were suffocating
or shrinking
and there were too many people
i wouldn't be able to fit
i'd get smashed
they were sucking up all the air!!

i would panic-stricken look up at the ceiling
and think about walking up there
where there are no people
where i can breathe my own air
and no one will shove me in the shoulder

and little tears would run down my face
and sometimes i couldn't breathe and i had to run into the
bathroom stall
and sit
and breathe again
and think of being all alone.

then it got worse
it became every day walking through the hallway
at school

i wore sunglasses and listened to music
to drown out their voices

and i was so happy when i saw someone
a friend
walking towards me
why are you wearing those glasses turn that down jeez
to talk to

but i never told anyone
because i thought it was fake
i thought i was overdramatizing

it was nothing.

then
the baseball game
when my mom
made me sit next to her on the bleachers
and little kids were crawling and kicking their feet
creating gigantic metallic echoes
that jolted my already overactive nerves

i put on my sunglasses
and tried listening to my music
but mom said turn it down
turn it down i can hear it
all of the screaming moms
screaming screaming moms
and little sticky kids sucking up all the sticky wet air

i had to get out of there
but she wouldn't let me leave
she said sit next to me
sit by your mother

but i had to get out of there
so i went to the bathroom
and sat in the smelly stall and little tears
ran down my cheeks
and i pouted the rest of the night
because i would much rather my mother
think i am a spoiled brat

than a *loony*
a crazy crazy loony with some crazy loony phobia

or even worse:
a *fake* loony

oohhhhhhh.

but!
i know it isn't fake!
i know it isn't fake.

my first drink

it is a dark night.

i know most nights are dark but this night is an especially dark one.

i'm not feeling up to it so i go in the kitchen
and take a beer from the fridge
and put it under my shirt where it is ice cold against my warm belly.

i go into the back room and lay on the ground and turn on the teevee
and watch late night cartoons and drink my beer.

it makes me feel a little sick at first but i get used to the feeling
real quick.

i have to.
i tell myself that i have to.

then when i still feel alright, i open the cabinet above the stove
and pull out a big heavy glass bottle.

i don't know what it is but i take a big ole mouthful of the stuff
and i swallow it down.

i immediately lean over the sink to throw up but nothing happens
and all the sudden i am very warm.

i walk outside and it is midnight.
i sit on the lawn.
i hear everything in the world in my ears then i

RUN!

i get up from my lawn and i RUN around the block and i jump and i skip
and when i am underneath a streetlamp i look at it:

oh. you should see it.
it is beautiful the way that streetlamp looks.

when i am looking up into it
i lose my balance and
i fall on my ass.

i start to giggle.
i giggle giggle giggle
then get up and skip and sprint at breakneck speed
around the neighborhood

giggling all the way.

and i can't stay up on the curb
i can't balance.

i can't walk the straight line on the road.

i can't stop giggling.

but in between giggles i am wishing that i'm not alone.
i am wishing that i'm not always so fucking *alone*.

i escape a lot.

before i "go to bed"

i take the collar off of my dog

so that when i open the door
to the backyard
she won't make big jangly noises

and wake my parents.

i take many walks around

the neighborhood.

drunk and alone.

the way that i dress
attracts attention
you could say.

i get compliments
each day and i get
dirty looks from black girls.

i shop at thrift stores now.
all of them.
i dig through the
racks and racks of trash and find
the treasures, baby.
the *treasures*.

i wear polka dots and plaid
and paisley and stripes
and florals and checks
and animal prints and sequins
and my very very favorite is houndstooth.

in the seventh grade i was a clown.
i wore striped knee socks and *beatles*
shirts. i wore glittery blue and green eyeshadows
and thick syrupy lip gloss.
i wore converse all stars and i
curled my hair.

in the eighth grade i was a grunge goddess.
i slept in hairspray so i could wake up
to a wonderful nest of matted hair.
i wore black *nirvana* tee shirts and torn jeans.
i switched my wire glasses to thick black
plastic. i ditched the green eyeshadow and picked
up the black eyeliner. my dad used to say i
looked like
ozzy osborne.
and i took that as a compliment.

now i am whatever i have become.

it is a wonderful thing to be yourself,
i suppose.

i just search through the racks and i pick out
piles and piles of clothes
and i feel them and i smell them and i stare at them
until i can decide which ones i can afford.
i wear skirts over pants. i wear flip flops and patterned flats
and my hair has become a long wavy light brown blanket
framing my face. i wear it up in paintbrushes and chopsticks
sometimes. but usually it is just long and wavy and wild and *there*.
i don't wear much makeup though lots of people tell me i should.
i wear coats over jackets over sweaters over tanktops. i wear skirts
over skirts. i wear shirts over dresses. and i wear SCARVES over EVERYTHING.

i like it all.

i get compliments
each day and i get
dirty looks from black girls.

when i am not sick and mom and dad are not tired and it is nobody's birthday,
i have to go to church.

at church i write anti-christ poems
and i draw sacrilegious pictures
and during the prayers i mumble curse words
and i never say "amen".

painting with turpentine

is so romantic
in my garage with the little worklamp
and the big wooden table and the rickety little chair
covered in blobs of paint
layers of blobs of paint.

the smell of turpentine makes it real
and the tchaikovsky playing from the corner
and the faint sound of the crickets outside
and the cool darkness

make it real.

and oh!

oh to be paid for this!

reading *vogue*

is always comforting.

finding beauty in hollow cheekbones

and ridiculous fashion trends.

nothing in a *vogue* is just direly important.

but everything is pretty enough to look at twice.

it is **ash wednesday** and daddy is out of town.

mom says we have to go to church it's ash wednesday.

i say but we NEVER go to church on ash wednesday.
and she says well we should. we certainly should.

i say i don't want to go.
i don't want that stupid cross on my head.

she says why not?
i say because.
because why?
because it's scary.

but she takes me anyway.
and the whole time i stare down at the program
staring at the part that scares me.
i don't want that stupid cross on my head.

i won't say any of the prayers.
i won't sing any of the hymns.
i won't look at anybody.
i just wait for it to be over.

then they sing the hymn right before
i start to cry and i can't help it.

then we walk slowly down the aisle and i can see what is going on here.

the preacher
he has a bowl of ashes in his hands.
I HAVE TO GET OUT OF HERE I HAVE TO GET OUT
and we are approaching
and his bowl is approaching and the ashes are approaching
and his black-stained fingers are approaching
and his smile is approaching and he speaks my name
and i look up at him
into his eyes
and his smile falters because i am crying.
he speaks my name again then says what he has to say.
something about God.
something about me.
something about something about something.
and i see his filthy fingers.
i see them dip into that bowl.
i see them reaching up towards my head
and i feel them labeling me
right in the middle of my fucking face
and i walk away very quickly to kneel at the altar
like everyone else
and i put my head down
in my hands like i am praying but
i am crying i am crying.

i wipe off that cross in the middle of church i wipe mine off.

i didn't want to come here.

i didn't want him to label me.

i told you i was scared.

and why didn't you *listen*?

i have to cheat at life
to get what i want

i have to steal to get the little things
i have to get high to feel nothing
i have to ditch school to have fun
i have to drink to be funny
i have to smoke cigarettes to look cool
i have to lie to be okay
i have to sneak out to feel free
i have to exaggerate to be interesting
i have to wear glasses to even see this fucking world
i have to
i have to
i have

after an art club meeting

(art club is the best; the people in art club are the best)

i go out into the parking lot with charlie and cara
out to cara's car.

i don't know why.

i don't know where we are going.

but i go and i sit in the back seat
and they sit in the front and start to smoke
cigarettes and i want one a lot.
i have always wanted one when they smoked
but i always thought i would sound stupid to be like

       hey? umm... can *i* try one of those?

so i never did.

but this time cara asks *me*.
and i say yes and i smile
and all of the D.A.R.E. classes and
drug dog/policeman duos that had visited my elementary schools
throughout the years
all the times i had been taught to JUST SAY NO flow through
my mind and right now i say:

yeah. sure.

so i smoke the silly cigarette.

have you ever had **that feeling** before you close your eyes
at night

that you will never wake up again?

have you ever had that feeling at school
in class

that you will never amount to anything?

have you ever had that feeling at home
in your tummy
deep in your tummy

that you are very, very empty?

the first time i did it

SMOKED POT THAT IS

i remember **one thing**
that haunts me still it does.

i remember them saying
okay now there's only time left for one thing
i remember chloe pulling a decorated box
out from under her bed
i remember rosemary's smile.

i remember the uncertainty in my tummy.
i can still feel it sometimes.

i saw them load the little pipe
and watched them take two hits.

i came and sat down on the bed
and took the pipe
and puffed on it.

and it hit me kind of hard in the back of the brain.
i felt alright.

i got up while they smoked some more
and looked at chloe's wall
plastered PLASTERED with
cut-outs of
vogue models so many pretty faces
and one of them she was so beautiful on the wall
spread her lips apart and smiled at me

then

i recognized her from somewhere
shit who IS that??

it
was

me.

i was gorgeous smiling there.
it was me looking into the mirror on her wall.
it was me.

i didn't
know what to
DO!!

i quickly turned away
and strode back to the mattress
and snatched the pipe from rosemary
and puffed on it
smoke from my nostrils
from my eyelids

i puffed on the pipe
like a little baby

staring off into nothing.

after we smoked it at chloe's
we went to the school play.

and chloe was in the stage crew so we got to go backstage
and we reeked of *cannabis sativa.*

the funny thing is that i was proud of myself.

and when i saw this one guy named eliot
he looked at me for
two seconds and then he said

are you *high?*

and i just giggled and giggled,
nodding my head like a madman.

he laughed and walked away.

chloe was doing makeup on the actors
and she said here.
here: do malachi.

okay.
malachi is this big fat jewish boy that
i have been in love with since
freshman year.

his curly black hair is beautiful
the way it splashes over his
horn-rimmed glasses.

and i love his stupid tee shirts
and i love his unkempt black beard
and his pasty skin
and i think he's the smartest person i've ever
met in my entire life.

but i was high.

rosemary and i were so *high*
and we were applying his makeup as he laughed
and talked with us.

when i was talking to malachi
i was ashamed
and i wondered very hard if he *knew.*

james
the school's favorite little pothead
looked me straight in the face and said
are you?

and i said yes.
(very seriously now.)

the farther this went the more i was regretting it.

but then the play started.

the play
was just

laughs
and it
was
too dark to even see a thing

i
think.

so
i think
so.

and charlie raised his eyebrows in my general
direction
so
i think so i think
so.

i smelled the marijuana
in my hair
all night long
and no my mother
didn't smell it
when she hugged me good night

and no
i didn't get caught
but something still wasn't right.

i could smell the marijuana
in my hair all night.

severely suicidal at least once a day
the rest of the time i'm wondering

how *could* you?

when i'm taking the most beautiful walk talking to
the most beautiful people listening to
the most beautiful music painting the most beautiful pictures

how *could* you want to die
how could you want out of this-
bliss?

then something happens and
like a bolt of lightning
it   *a l l*   comes back to me

oh .

this is what i hate
this is hate
this is hate
it is black and red smears across my eyes
it is choking me and saying
take over for me

just finish the job

it's your only way out
it's your only way out

this is when i only see the world as ugly
and gruesome and mean.

this is when the tears won't stop coming
and the eyes won't stop puffing and the nose
won't stop stuffing and the ears can't hear nothing

because the anger and the hate have taken over
and all i want is to die

this is when:

i can think of nothing but   the knife
                             the knife
                             of the end of my life.

i really creep myself out sometimes

i read this stuff the day after
and it's so disgusting and chilling and strange and gruesome

but i can't deny that i felt it so honestly
so i try to ignore it

but i can't
and i think maybe i'm crazy
or bipolar
or something

or there's another personality that comes out when
i get so
angry

or maybe i really truly do

want to die.

i don't know what it is about chloe
but even though she smokes
and even though she lies
she is the best person in the universe.

every time i see her
my eyes light up and something
inside of me says OH BOY
and i'm all ready to have a blast.

she is **my very favorite bad influence.**

my **hair** is long

real long.

it's fuzzy and curly and wavy and brown and blonde
and crawling down my back
like ivy.

but

i think i'm going to cut it all off.

i have smoked from a soda can
i have smoked from a pipe
but today:

it is bong time.

buh-bong time.

we lean over it and it is cheap
and plastic and blue
and it smells like shit
and we breathe in and it bubbles
and the smoke goes into our bodies
and we lean back
onto the bed
laying all over chloe's big black dogs
who lick our faces with their massive tongues
and we laugh and laugh and laugh
and rings of smoke
come out of our mouths
and our nostrils

and our ears.

i remember the best day of my life.

it was such a good day.
it was pretty outside and rosemary had asked me to ditch.

i said fine even though we were in front of my good friend wayne
and for some reason i always feel like i should protect my good friend wayne
from that part of myself.

that part of myself that gets drunk at night.

but i said yes and when i got into charlie's car i looked around
and there they were.

the greatest people.
the most marvelous wonderful people.

there was rosemary and chloe, charlie and cara.

and there was me in the middle of that backseat
encompassed in them all.
i remember how chloe handed me a cigarette because
i had smoked one before with her and she remembered and she kind of looked proud when
she watched me light it and i kind of felt proud when i exhaled that punk-ass perfume
through my nostrils and mouth and all of me felt invincible.

i rolled down my window and flicked the ash and smiled that i had flicked the ash.
i had flicked the ash.

i looked very 50s dahling.
i was wearing this red and white polka-dot dress.
i looked very glamorous smoking a cigarette charlie told me so.

we went to hobby lobby to get a canvas then we drove around and smoked cigarettes
            then we got out and walked around in this gorgeous neighborhood called
"crown heights"
and we smoked cigarettes and it felt so good as i strolled
down the street pointed out houses with these people
these marvelous people
and flicking this ash from my cigarette.
my cigarette.

we pointed out houses we wanted to buy
then we went to the blue cup i FINALLY went to that chic little coffee house, *the blue cup* i bet
charlie doesn't know
that i've been waiting for this day.

he gets the greatest coffee and it's called a *raspberry decadence* and
it means so much when he lets me have a sip
because i've been waiting for this day.

an aimless cat walks up to us and wants some of charlie's sandwich.

it was the best day of my life.

i did it.

i went over to kelsey's.

they put it in a **ponytail**
and kelsey held the scissors
and i heard
the
sound
and then

my head was lighter
and my neck was cold.

i was holding a tail of hair in my hand.
a tail.

this came off of my head.

this used to be attached to my head.

(what have i done??)

"do you like it?"

yeah.
it looks great.

i'm working on this portrait
of this girl i know, jenny harcourt

and it's looking good

i carry
the pencil sketch of her face
on a big stretched canvas
to school
and show it (off) to her

and all the black kids in my math class
cover their mouths and lean back in their seats and
say ooooooooooooooooooooooooh shit

because it looks just like her

and people in the hallway that i
don't even know
say
hey is that jenny harcourt

and i say
yes
yes it is

but when i look at it

all i see is a bunch of muddy pencil smudges

i am **obsessive compulsive** about playing solitaire
and trying to solve rubik's cubes.

there is something so simple about solving something like that
that it makes me feel like i can solve anything.

i have gotten to where i can win a game of solitaire in less than 2 minutes.
you should see me at it.

i have started carrying around my rubik's cube.
to school
to the grocery store
to orchestra rehearsals
to band practice
to assemblies
in my bed at night

awake.

trying to solve it.

I KNOW I CAN SOLVE IT I *KNOW* I CAN SOLVE IT

hoping.

that if i solve this

then everything else will be solved,

then i will have found the answer.
it's right here.
it's *right* here.

once in math
i **solved** the whole green side of my rubik's cube
and i was so happy

then this black kid said here let me have it
and he started jumbling it all up
saying it's okay i can fix it
and i felt my stomach twisting and churning watching him do that
so i turned away.

then he gave up and handed me my cube.
i looked at it.

in the palm of my hand there it was.

the greens were scattered *every*where.

i sleep with a lot of pillows

and kelsey only sleeps with one.

i can eat one marshmallow

and kelsey can eat a ton.

i don't like peanut butter

but kelsey likes it a lot.

kelsey is often beautiful

and i am often not.

the love tunnel is part of the sewage system i think.
funny... something with such a beautiful name that is a
part of something so well-known for being dirty and gross and ugly.
sewage.

it is just a big cement ditch adjacent to my old middle school
and i discovered it with a red-headed boy named max
when i was in the seventh grade.

and he held my hand and
he made me keep going
he was behind me and we were
walking through it
and i just kept walking
even though it was pitch dark
and wet
even though i kept saying not yet not yet
he said c'mon it's fun
it never hurt anyone
so just go.

and afterwards i am *enthralled.*

i take rosemary there.
we paint all the walls.
we paint each other.
we paint big and colorful
right outside the tunnel
"THE LOVE TUNNEL"
so that everyone knows it is there.
a construction worker sees us
and says "does the city know you're doing this?"
and rosemary looks him straight in the face
and says "no."
and he tells us we have to stop someone could call
the police
so when he leaves we crawl inside the tunnel and
paint some more
where he can't see us.

i take kelsey there.
i photograph her delicate features
against the harshness of graffiti and obscenities.
she puts a big brown and white bow on her head.
she looks into the shutter.
i make her laugh and her smile
makes me smile and the camera clicks.
i make a short film from the pictures
and it is a really good one.

i take charlie there.
we sneak onto the construction site
for the new wing of the middle school.
charlie has his vintage camera for
photography class and he tries to
photograph me in the tunnel
but i can't keep a straight face-
i remember it was SO hard.
we take pictures of little orange flags
and pipes sticking out of the red dirt
and stacks of dirty bricks
and half-up walls
and roofless rooms
and then we chase an ice cream truck
all the way back to my house.

i made a picture for this boy named dallas.

he's big and tall
and his hair is long and black and he listens to *the ramones*.

i like him.

what i made,
well
it's a picture of an alien and
next to the alien it says
DALLAS

but when i gave it to him
it was pretty awkward.

he was like

............thanks...

and i was like

.........alright...

and then i went back to my lunch table
with kelsey and i giggled and giggled

at me.

i'm getting this little tiny space

between my two front teeth

and i can't tell

if i like it   or if i hate it

because sometimes

it's kind of cute   it's kind of hideous

so i shove on my retainer

and hope for the best

maybe it will go away forever

my english teacher has the loudest goddamned voice

on the whole planet

and when i am hung over it is fucking un*bear*able

so i cover my ears when she speaks

and once this smart girl looked over at me

at the circles under my eyes

and the hands cupping my ears

the rebellion.

she gasped and
turned away.

the *nerve.*

i looked into the mirror
and i said to myself:

i fucking *hate* you.

i hate you.

you are ugly.

you are stupid.

you fuck-up.

you big fuck-up.

you're crazy, you know.

you're fucking *crazy.*

i'm going to *kill* you.

i'm going to fucking stab you to death.

*every*one fucking hates you.

i hate you *so much.*

i said all of that out loud.
to myself.
into the mirror.
i really did.

this is one of those times when i'm chastising my brain
for hating myself
for wanting to die
for killing the part of me that right now is so very very happy

listening to this band from iceland
called *sigur ros*
(that means "victory rose", did you know?)
petting my cat
just got back from kelsey's house
where everything seemed just
like *old times*

we watched a sappy romantic comedy
and when i laid my head on her shoulder
i felt the same warmth
and when she put her hand on my knee
she felt the same warmth
and she had the same loud laugh that she always had

how could i not want this
how come at night
alone
everything good melts away
and all that is left is hate
black and red
and knives
and tears

why can't i always be this happy?

once when my parents were asleep

i woke up
and went into the garage and painted
with my oil paints

i painted my mom's face
smiling and laughing with her best friend.

i drank two beers and some vodka shots.

then i called charlie and talked to him about charles manson
and murder and pudding and things like that.

i didn't really want to stop talking to him
even after it had been two hours.

sometimes that would happen,
we would talk that long.

and neither of us would really know when it was
time to say

okay, well... i guess i'll talk to you later.

sometimes

i really love my parents

when they come into my dark room
and i am crying and curling into a ball
and pulling my hair
and ugly snot is running down my ugly face
and i can't stop making this awful sound
and i can't stop these awful tears from falling

so they hold me still until i am okay
they say they love me
they say it will get better

i can't stop crying
because i am in that dark place
that i fear i will never escape from

but just hearing fake condolences
makes it a little bit easier

waking up in the morning

is always a surprise
i never know if i'm going to still be
puffy bulging red eyed

or if my face will show no
signs of struggle

and again when my friends see me in the hallways and ask

how are you

i can still say

fine
or
good
or
swell

when i haven't felt that way
since

since...

?

one eye's red
on the side of my head
and i think that i'm dead
but i'm not dead yet

my face is green
and my parakeet is mean
and i'm shouting obscene
but i'm not dead yet

one leg's numb
and my brain is so dumb
i just stepped on some gum
oh, i'm not dead yet

my mouth is dry
but the tears that i cry
will fall from my eye
because i'm not dead yet

oh i'm not dead yet
not yet
not yet not
yet

daddy got some new vodka

it's from finland
and the bottle is frosty clear
and from the bottom a swirl of red blooms
inside of the glass.
it is Raspberry Fusion flavored
and it tastes
like sugary acid.

but after i swallow it down
it feels first like a campfire
then like a very soft candle
burning inside of my tummy.

but at the bus stop this morning
the candle has gotten meaner
not so soft
and then it isn't even a candle anymore.
it is a hammer.
it is a huge hammer and it crawls
up my arms
and into my head
where it bashes in my skull

repeatedly
repeatedly.

i try to do **sit-ups** in the middle of the night
sometimes even at dawn
because i have a tiny little belly
the kind that lazy artists get
the kind that happen to people
who never get up and do something
unless it's get a pencil or use the telephone
or turn up the radio.

i try to make it go away
but it won't
and the next day my whole stomach
is sore
and the next day it is a rock
and the next day it is an artist's belly again.

and i forget about it for a little while.

**this boy on my bus
is cute**

he waits at my bus stop
with me.

at first i hated that because
i was used to being alone it was awkward we never talked but today-

it is freezing.

i walk up to the stop talking
to myself when i see his legs
behind this tree
i giggle all
i can see are his feet his
jeans his
ipod and his
hands holding it.
turning it off.

he spits into the grass.
i can't see his face.
i smile.

a BLAST of cold wind hits
my face and burns my eyes and freezes my toes.

but he is behind that silly tree. the wind doesn't hit him.

i like him.
he is smart.

another gust of wind-
it hurts
it is too cold
i run to him

behind that tree
and I say

"hi Jesus it's fucking cold"
and he smiles
so cute
and i smile
stand beside him.

he shifts on his feet
and pretends to listen to his ipod but
i know that it is turned off.

i listen to him breathe.

the bus comes.
we smile relief and get on he
sits across from me
and props his feet on my seat.

i fall asleep.

i hate **pep** assemblies.

i just try and find someone i know to sit by

so i can try and be witty and composed

during something so mindbustingly embarrassing

as being a part of something like this.

this yelling

the cheerleaders

the sports teams

the people

THERE ARE SO MANY PEOPLE!

i can't breathe but

there is nothing i can do about it

so i turn to chloe

sitting next to me

and we start to make fun

of the people around us,

denying that we are a part of it.

at school i am inside of a shell

like a little turtle

and i only come out

for people i like

although i don't even like

the people that i like

because i don't like *anyone*.

i especially don't like me.

i especially do not like me.

but i am always in the shell with myself.

i will never go away no matter

how many times i try to lose myself

always when i go back into my shell

i am still there.

i am still there.

horror movies
like

poltergeist
and *rosemary's baby*

what's the matter with helen?
and *psycho*

make me feel like maybe my life isn't that bad.

i could have been sucked into my closet
or be giving birth to satan's spawn.

i could be rooming with a crazy woman
who cuts up my rabbits or
i could be murdered naked in a shower.

i guess being a little nuts is not much of a big deal
compared to that stuff.

this year has been eight years
this week has been months.

i can't believe i'm living like this.
i can't believe i haven't collapsed in the middle of the street.
i can't believe i haven't gotten caught.
i can't believe my luck.
i can't believe how horrible this has all turned out.

paisley collection

is the name of a band.

my band.

me and charlie's band.

me and charlie and rosemary and jon and alex and scot's band.

we play shows.

you should come to one some time.

i'm always making flyers.

do you want to see them?

we have a cd.

would you like to buy a cd?

this band-

my

band-

is the sole purpose of my life.

and if they ever say it again-

if they EVER say i can't play with this band-

i am going to kill myself

(because there *is* nothing else)

and they will be *soo* sorry.

do you read vonnegut?

barely anyone my age does.

i do.

i like to discuss his writing
with whomever i can.

i like to share his novels with
the world.

he's so hilarious i swear
PLEASE read it.

please read this book.

it's so good i promise you.

and sadly

they never listen.

sadly

they never do.

i still cry in the shower

so that i won't be able to tell my tears from the water

so that my mother won't hear me
so that my mother won't hear me

we have a show
the band and i
and i don't get to stay
i don't know why
but after we play
i have to say goodbye

and hop in the car with my parents.

our show is
at the conservatory
i stand
with quentin
the boy i build up in my head
to be a hero

and another guy
older
a stranger
who is handsome
and blows smoke
into my face in a
friendly sort of way

and we watch ricky allen play.

and the stranger looks at quentin
and says

damn this guy's real good.

and i smile then run to the bathroom
and throw up

all over the toilet seat.

proof that i'm crazy:

sometimes i wake up in the middle of the night and eat a bowl of oatmeal.

sometimes i sleep on the floor.

sometimes i walk round at midnight.

sometimes i get in a big fight

with myself.

sometimes i get nauseous

at the smells.

sometimes i get a headache

with the sounds.

sometimes i get nightmares

from the clowns.

did i tell you i am terribly afraid of birds?
mostly black ones.
big black crows
i am so scared of them
and i especially hate it on hot days
when they walk around with
their mouths wide open it is absolutely
vile.

i am still experiencing this irrational fear
of people
crowds
big rooms
loud talking

esp.: cafeterias, restaurants, rock concerts, orchestra recitals, sports games, shopping
            malls, schools, festivals of any sort, assemblies, and occasionally even
            moderately small club meetings.

i log onto the computer
search for a list of phobias
and look up "crowds"
and it comes up with a big ugly word
AGORAPHOBIA

and it explains the symptoms
and they were exactly the sum of ME

i exhale relief
and inhale anxiety
printing off the information.
i read it all night
over and over in my bed,
crying about the reality of it all.

next day i randomly say to mom:
do you have any phobias?

she says
ahhhhhh, well.
i dunno.
i'm afraid of dying, i guess.

oh,
i say.
i'm afraid of large crowds.
i get really nervous.

she turns up the radio.

i look out the window.

oh.

chugging down a *monster* **energy drink**

i feel at home inside myself

with sugar vibrating all inside

and this is how i felt

when i was alive.

and people laugh at me when

i say

"mmm... tastes like memories."

but i am so serious.

monster energy drink tastes

like my life and it makes

me feel like i am artificially

living it again.

at the bus stop i ask the cute boy if he has a cigarette
because i am dying for one.

his eyes light up like a fire
and he smiles to himself.

he looks back up at me like i am
a completely different person
and says

no. i smoked my last one this morning.

i don't feel like going to class today.

so when i get to my second block
i take a bathroom pass
and i go to the bathroom

for about an hour
until i fall **asleep in the stall**

it's great
as long as
i'm
away
from
it all.

i hate the way i look.

i know i shouldn't.

i know it's wrong.

people tell me that i'm pretty sometimes.

but **i never believe it**.

because

i know they're wrong

because

my skin is awful and

my face is serious

and my eyes are little and

my hips are big

and my tummy is growing and

my face is getting rounder

and my nails are all ragged and torn.

it's so sad to hate yourself.

your *self*.

it is something that should not be hated

and it is something that should not be cried over

and it is not something to be ashamed of

and i've heard all that crap about self-esteem

but what about for REAL?

my mom comes in

when i'm writing a poem
and i cover it up real quick

for obvious reasons
and she gets all offended
and says you don't have to do that
and stomps
out

so i finish my poem and i get up
to go talk to her

but everybody is gone
and i don't know where they went
the house is empty

i sit on my bed
and rock back and forth
and wonder

why am i such a horrible daughter?

i'm just a big fat **baby**

that's all

i remember once

when i was freaking out
having a little baby fit

i wondered if Jesus was real

i yelled at my ceiling

GOD

GOOOOD

if you are there
then

kill me now

and i waited and cried

GOD KILL ME NOW

and he didn't

and i knew that he wasn't real
because i was really hurting here
and he didn't give a shit

i used to listen to *the beatles*
and then

nirvana and *green day*

and then the *starlight mints*
and then *fiery furnaces*

and then

sufjan stevens and *joanna newsom*

and then *devendra banhart* and

now i just listen to

the *pixies*, the *pixies*, the *pixies*.

the screaming motherfucking *pixies*.

when mom is getting ready in the mornings
i pour pure vodka into my *lion king* thermos
that i always carry to school.

but i used to fill it with coffee.

or herbal tea.

at the talent show rehearsal
rosemary wants to **brush her teeth**

so we both go into the bathroom
and as she brushes her teeth

i say

do you have any scissors?

she says

yeah.

i say

wanna cut my hair some more?

she says

YEAH

so she gets them out of her bag
and we sit cross-legged on the floor
and pick random pieces to cut
and it feels so good.

we can hear someone playing piano onstage.
it is good spur-of-the-moment hair cutting music.

if there is such a thing.

when we are done
there is hair
all down the back of my dress

and it is covering the bathroom floor.

we leave the room giggling like madwomen
and run outside to show charlie.

my agoraphobia kicks in
at **the talent show**

i look at charlie one more time
and he comforts me with his smile
and i snuggle my chin into my violin
and wiggle my finger a little bit.
then before i am ready
the curtain is up-

and it is us on stage.

the lights are so bright.

and we play.

the show goes well but
it is just **the first show**
tomorrow will be bigger
tomorrow will be better

rosemary says
              you wanna go smoke something
                          and i say
                                         sure
she says
              what do you wanna smoke cigarettes or-
                              -cigarettes.
and we get in her car
and i smoke mine
and still
STILL
i don't know why it feels
so wonderful
to exhale smoke
from my nostrils.

STILL i can't explain it.
but i won't deny the feeling.
            i won't deny the beauty.
                        i won't deny the truth.

we win
-second place-
(not bad, not bad)

and charlie makes me carry around the trophy
because it is so huge and it makes him
feel like an asshole

i make my parents mad by manipulating
them into letting me go out with the band
afterwards
but i don't care.
i'm not really going out with the band.
i think the rest of the band is just going to smoke pot and i don't feel like it.
so i just go out with charlie.

and we drive around listening to the song
HOLLA BACK GIRL
turned up really loud
the way regular teenagers would
and we bounce a little in our seats
with excitement and excessive bass beats.

we get slush-puppies and we stop
to drop off some equipment or something
at some kid's house slurping our brain-freezes
and then he pretty much
just takes me home.

but it was fun.

it was really fun.

especially the HOLLA BACK GIRL part
and The Asshole Trophy.

i take **long baths** sometimes and listen to *sigur ros*
because charlie once told me that i should try it.

i did and i've done it ever since.

i make lots of bubbles that smell like pretend
and i put them on the tippy-top of my head.

i play the cd and sink down into a bubbly fortress.

then when i am trying to relax,
i start to notice the time passing by.

the water dripping from the faucet.
the water slowly getting cold.
the bubbles popping.
i can hear them in my ears!
i can hear the bubbles popping in my ears!
the water evaporating.
the water being sucked away from me by some unknown force,
and it's stealing the water from me!

it's stealing my minutes!
how many minutes of mine have been STOLEN this way?

what am i doing here?!

i get up out of the bathtub
and jump into my bed
soaking wet
and without clothes
and cover myself up with the blanket.

two hours later i wake up naked and dry.

i've started throwing up a lot.

not on *purpose* for God's sakes.

i don't know why it's happening.

but it happens a lot now.

when i laugh too hard

or right after i eat.

when i get a little bit nervous

or a whole lot relieved.

when i'm just brushing my teeth.

my mom is making me

feel like some kind of criminal

for vomiting.

i am not bulimic.

Jesus.

that's gross.

i'm always wanting to say things to charlie.

i don't know what it is
about him

but he's amazing.

i don't want to tell him
because i don't want him to know.

if he knew
that he was amazing
then all of the mystery would be gone.

he and i have been friends for
quite sometime.
we were even friends before we were friends.

we are almost exactly the same person.
and we still don't know just how close we are.

i want to live with him someday.
i don't want to have his children.
i don't want to marry him.

i just want to run away with him
to *be* with him
in his band
i want us to paint together
and be real close
and groggily sip coffee on early mornings.

because we could do that
we could manage it.

we've talked about it
randomly.

when he drives me back
after he buys me a sno-cone and we listen to the *starlight mints* windows down
i think about it.
he talks about living in norman.

we should live in norman.
and other times it's happened-

hey we should live in that house right there   he points out the window
will you help me buy it   i ask him smiling at his curly hair in the wind,
                                                       he dyed it red you know
sure i will   he takes a big slurp of his sno-cone -
                                                                spills it down his front
then it's settled   i take a sip of mine and it leaks onto my hand

that's when we laugh.

that's when i wonder if he's serious.

that's when i wonder if he's ever as serious as me.

that's when i wonder if he knows that i'm crazy.

the battle of the bands

i have a lot of fun
we play great
i get a sno-cone with charlie
we play barefoot

i get to wear jack allen's hat
i get to wear jack allen's hat

he's funny
he's a spaz
i like talking to him

we don't win

and i don't get to see the *starlight mints*
but it's okay.

until i get home.
then everything is ugly again.

i forgot to call my mom an hour ago.
i fucked up again.

they yell at me again.
same old same old.

i tried to ignore it but once they leave me alone
i go hysterical i have a fit alone in my room
i tell myself just what i am going to do to
myself and why i deserve it

when my dad comes in and my silent sobs
get louder

why are you crying

crycrycrycrycrycrycrycry

huh? why?

crycrycrycrycrycrycry

and for the first time
it is my *dad* who is holding me
he holds me so tight
so that he will keep me together
because we both know that i am falling apart
but he holds all my pieces together in a big daddy bear hug
and he holds me until i stop crying
and i know that he doesn't care that i am getting snot and tears and drool
all over him so i slowly calm down

he says
i love you go take a shower

and i feel a little better
because it is finally him
he tapes me together
and i know it won't hold for long
but at least for a little while
i won't be falling apart

ever since they said I couldn't play the *paisley collection* show
i have started having **chronic nightmares**.

they are full of death.
they are full of big gray spiders.

and now
when i close my eyes when i am awake
i imagine ten thousand bullets being shot into my chest.
i imagine a dagger sticking into my face.
i imagine a noose tight around my neck.
sucking on the underside of a pillow for air.
swallowing the eightieth aspirin.
jumping off the bridge.

then i start seeing things when my eyes are open.

i am driving with my mom
to violin lessons i see **two cats**
sitting in someone's lawn
and they both look exactly like my cat
and i say hey mom look at that!!

but then we drive past them
and i can see that they aren't cats at all.
they are two little... pinwheels.
spinning round and round.
rainbow colored
sticking from the grass.

they aren't cats at all.

and my mother says

what? look at what?

a girl walks towards charlie and i
in the hallway

i am reading her shirt
and at first it says something
and then the words
move around
and **twist and twirl**
and then her shirt says something else.
something entirely different.

i look at charlie.

he didn't even notice.

what gives?

drink
drink
drink

while there's still beer here

drink drink drink
don't let your throw-up splash
in the sink

just drink
drink drink

then you won't have to
think
think
think

(wink, wink)

i want to **cut** myself.

do you think it will hurt?

i've been thinking about how

jack allen

let me wear his hat

how he turned around
and saw it on my head

how he's just a little bit taller than me

and he said goofy faced

have *you* seen that girl who
stole my hat

and he took it away from me
ten minutes later

and inside i wanted it to stay

and then he put it right back on my head

until he left when he ran by with dallas
(i used to like dallas i used to like dallas)
and snatched it off my head

and smiled
he turned the corner

and he was gone

i eat lunch in rosemary's art room
with her and this cool chick
named cara.

i think cara is funny because she listens
to bands like *styx* and *journey* and *reo speedwagon*.
that's funny to me.

so i just carry my lunch in there
(because usually by lunchtime
kelsey and i are so sick of each other)
and i pretend i am an art student

and i fall in love with life
until the bell rings.

i am sitting in english class

and i just now finished this really good book called

the perks of being a wallflower by stephen chbosky
and it was just so good
that immediately i started back at the
beginning reading it again.

it helped me forget.

for those 9 hours straight reading it,

it helped me forget.

in the summertime:

i used to make myself margaritas and cheesecake.

i told benjamin they were virgins
and he believed me
while his eyes were glued to the teevee
the tequila spilled in
and i salted the rims
and said
PAAARTAAY
and benjamin laughed
thought i was funny
thought i was cool
i hope.

and we laughed
and laughed
and turned up the music too loud
and walked places we weren't supposed to
like the two miles to hobby lobby so i could
get a little tube of paint
and the mile and a half just to get a sno-cone
that melted by the time you got back.

but we had fun.

the summer days
when i used to make myself
margaritas
and
cheesecake.

once upon a time my little brother benjamin
and i
in the midst of a broiling summer heat wave
walked all the way to a sandwich shop
and ate sandwiches
and then we walked to a movie-rental
and rented *tale of two sisters*
(this creepy asian horror film)
and POLTERGEIST
(one of my very favorites)
and BREAKFAST OF CHAMPIONS
(movie version of a kurt vonnegut book- bound to be interesting)
then we walked to the party store and i bought groucho marx
glasses you know the
ones with the big nose
and the hairy eyebrows?
and benjamin bought a mardi gras mask
and wore it the whole walk home
though it made his face break out
in a cold sweat he said
i look neat in it.
i look neat.

and we crossed the busy street.
walking so many miles that day.

when we got home we took freezing cold
showers dang it's hot out there
tell me about it.

then we watched horror movies and benjamin
hid them under his bed when mom got home.

then **it came time** to turn them in
(the secret movies)
we have to turn them in before mom
and daddy find out says benjamin

but when?
but when?

then
benjamin is gone with mom and dad
it's raining so hard out
but it's my only chance
so i stick my favorite gray hat atop my head
and get on my bike
and head out with the movies in a
purse across my chest.

already soaking wet by the time i
pass ricky allen's house and wave-
he sees me riding in the rain as
he gets out of his car probably
thinking
what a crazy girl

not crazy in a good way
crazy in a CRAZY way

but i rode on.

i remember how hard it was.
i remember how in the middle of
the expressway i almost passed out
because my legs were pumping too fast
and my skin was too cold and my head
was getting lighter and lighter and floating away
from my body.

i remember the concerned look on a lady's face
as she almost ran me over with her crown victoria.

i was so wet.
the rain was falling so hard.
my legs were so tired.

i got there, though.
i got back, though.

and i was okay.
and the movies were returned.

but the next day i was sick as death.

sometimes **i miss things** too much.

i miss things that have already happened.
things that will never happen again.

i miss the day when all the lights went out in the school
and me and charlie were in ms. sim's class
and we got to share this candle that smelled like lies.

i miss mrs. kyle's class because some of the things that she said
were just...
RIDICULOUS.
so ridiculous.
i miss laughing at that.
i miss laughing and saying, "oh, *boy*. that's ri*dic*ulous."

i miss me and rosemary pushing our desks together in history class
and getting made fun of for wearing peejay pants every day of the week.

i miss writing long long notes to charlie
and getting long long responses.

i even miss texas sometimes.

i used to live in texas.

sometimes i even miss texas.

i left my vodka thermos in english class
and i am panicking
because i just realized that i had left it.

it has my name on the lid.
it is right beside my desk in there.
and it is full to the brim with pure vodka.

i am rushing out of my third block
and banging on the door of my english class
i am looking next to my desk.

oh God where is it oh God

and it is still there.

i walk over to it calmly but quickly
and pick it up
and leave the room
shutting the door behind me
and taking a
nice
big
swig.

do you ever just wiggle
your fingers
and watch the bones
move

and think

goddammit i am just
a fucking *machine*

?

i start **riding home** with lena every now and then
because i like dallas
and he carpools with her
and he is so funny
when he tries to fit his huge self
in her tiny little back seat.

i laugh and laugh
and blush and blush
because i always fall for
boys who don't give
a shit and they never give a shit
about
me.

i have the cutest little dog you could ever imagine.

she's a little rat terrier
her face is slowly turning gray
and her name is speck.

like pee wee herman's puppy.

i like the way she licks my leg
in the middle of the night.

i like the way she jumps and scratches
i like the way she doesn't bite.

i like the way she'll eat whatever
you put inside her bowl.
i like the way she'll put her bone inside
a dug-up hole.

i like the way she'll run away
if the gate is left unclosed
but if you call her name she'll run right to you,
predisposed.

i'm still **cutting my** hair.

when i get bored.

when i get lonely.

when i get tired of the monotony of my life.

my hair can always be different.

and i like the sound the scissors make
and the shape of the hole for my fingers.

and i like the way it feels when hair falls down to the floor
and the effect of cutting it piece by piece.

can't reach it in the back.
can't reach it in the back.

SNIP.

i used to let **mom read**
some of this stuff.

some of the less-controversial ones.

but then she would FIND a little bit of controversy
in between the lines
and she would inject it with assumptions
and it would grow grow GROW
into something huge.

and she would say that there was too much cursing.
i think the fucking cursing adds character.

i think the fucking cursing adds passion.

i fucking curse all day long in my head
and my writing is going to fucking curse just like me.

i feel guilty for this one time
when kelsey spent the night.

we had gone to a chic little venue/coffeehouse/artist's lounge
and painted and talked and listened to soothing acoustic music.

we had painted together in the garage-
(something i had been wanting to do for such a long time)
i had painted sunshine, she clara bow.

it was all-in-all a very grandiose evening.
and,
wallowing in this,
i sat on the countertop
my mother was asleep
kelsey was right across from me

as we drank soda
and tried to pay attention
to how loud we were giggling.

that's when i went from being on the countertop
to being in the sink.

i had slid into it accidentally and i was laughing
so loudly and violently over this that i was making no sound.
kelsey too was cracking up in that kelsey sort of way
and she came to join me
and we both sat there in the sink and smiled
contentedly swallowing our cokes and potato chips
when one of us hit the faucet with our elbows
and the sink turned on
and we both felt the cold running water splash our thighs
so
we jumped out
and stood on the kitchen floor
exploding into fits of laughter
and oh my God i couldn't believe it.

i was laughing so hard that i thought i would die.
i hadn't laughed in months.
this was... oh this was too good to be true.

that's when my mom woke up in her bed
that's when my stomach started hurting
and i ran to the bathroom
still laughing as i threw up into the toilet
i still laughed and laughed and my mother knocked on the door

yelling

CHELSEA WHAT ARE YOU *DOING* IN THERE???

and i still feel
that i am responsible for ruining such a nice evening with my throw-up.

so i hope that the both of them would pretty please forgive me for that.

have i told you about **my disguise**?

i wear a big big huge lumpy scarf and a long skirt over baggy jeans.
i wear a fuzzy gray hat with a bill that juts out, shadowing my face.
i wear big huge dark sunglasses over my puffy eyes.
i wear a long-sleeved super-heavy knit sweater and i hide my hands inside.
i wear my worn-since-seventh-grade converse.
i wear headphones over my ears playing the *pixies*.

i walk down the halls and sip vodka
and pretend that nobody notices i'm there.

the knife
the knife
the end of my life

i wish i could play the piano
i wish i could play the guitar

but most of all...

my very innermost dream...

is to have a harp.

a colossal majestic towering harp
with strings out the wazoo
and pedals and a cushiony bench.

i want this more than i want hair on my head.
i want this more than i want most anything.

oh, what a dream.

the harp is such a marvelous thing.

rosemary and shane and this badass girl named jane
and this other badass girl named jamie
and well ME
all ditch fourth block today
to go smoke pot but rosemary's dealer
won't provide the stuff
so we end up just driving around
waiting for him to call back
listening to the pixies
and i am fortunate enough to sit shotgun the whole time
with the *lovely* rosemary
so we can sing all the songs together.

shane keeps trying to get people in
convenient stores to buy him
cigarettes but nobody would
and we laugh.

we go to his house
(and i feel kind of badass
with these badass girls)
and we light firecrackers
in shane's driveway
and i don't know why
we are doing this.

but one goes off
in his cat's water bowl and it
is magnificent
the way it

splashes!

today i paint on black eyeliner
just to see what it feels like

and it feels alright.

and i put on my disguise
and i fill up my vodka thermos
and i walk to the bus stop

bundled up and sipping liquor.

what if Jesus

is real

and i'm going to hell

oh well
there's nothing i can do now

i want to die

i want to go to heaven

but **i think**

i think

i need to know

if i believe in that

first

i think

i don't think

i want

to think

anymore

rosemary drives me home
and this guy named heath.

he has three cigarettes and we all smoke one
as she drives.

he looks at me and says
"you don't look like you would smoke."

i say why although i know it is true.

"i dunno you just look like **a good person**."

and i do not take that as a compliment.
i frown out the window and puff on that fucking cigarette.

i can be a smoker too asshole

questions

at what point does it become unhealthy to sniff turpentine?

how many sniffs does it take to consider it "abuse"?

at what point does one become an alcoholic?

and how many cigarettes does it take to get hooked?

there are only a couple of songs
that i've played in orchestra
in my whole life
that have made me feel

like
THIS IS WHY

why what?
well, why *every*thing.

why everything *is*.

songs like
in the hall of the mountain king
and
beethoven's fourth, i think it was.

oh it was so beautiful

and

the phantom of the opera

and

well those are the only ones i can remember.

those are the songs that are why
everything *is*.

when you play them
you can feel it
swimming around
in your blood

and your blood
likes it.

lena and i

stole a lot of things
on this orchestra trip.

we went to dallas in a big fancy bus.
and we felt really cool stuffing things into our pockets.
we did.

and...

she's such a good friend that
she didn't tell on me.
she took all the blame

just so i could play the paisley collection show.

but i'm so very glad because
deep inside i was afraid that
i would kill myself if i missed another show.

that it might have been the last freakin' straw
because i just love that stupid band

waay

too

much.

when mom and dad
find out that
i have an unexcused absence
they sit me down on the couch
and i feel like clawing at my throat
because i can't escape from this
situation.

they **dig it out** of me.

they dig it all up.

my parents know all now.
they know about the pot,
about the liquor.
about the ditching about the sadness.

and the tears start flowing.
they BURST
and now i am a great big geyser
in the middle of the living room
exploding and breaking down
into hysterics
and i try to walk back into my room
but i see great big gray spiders crawling
all over my door
so i run and fall onto my mom's bed
where she puts a cold rag on my head
and tells me everything will be okay.
i try to talk to her but my words aren't coming out right
she doesn't know what the hell i am saying
and by the size of her eyes i know i am frightening her.

who poured the tainted blood into my veins?
who blew the polluted wind into my lungs?
who planted the measly hairs inside my head?
who connected the feeble bones under my skin?

who *did* that?

there are some really nice people **in the world**

and some of them are really repulsive.

there are some really beautiful things in the world

and some of them are really vicious.

there are so many things to do in the world

but how can one do them all?

so why should i live at all?

i
like
to
pop
my
fingers
and
my
toes
and
my
ankles
and
my
wrists
and
my
neck
and
my
back
and
my
knees
because
it
feels
really
good.

mom and dad **think that i am anemic**
or something
because i keep throwing up so much

so i have to go to the doctor and stuff
so i can get tested to see what the hell is wrong
with me.

at the doctor he says
what seems to be the problem

well i've been throwing up a lot
and i'm not sick.

my dad says
but she's been very stressed out

and i say
yeah i have.

would you like to tell me about that
the doctor says.

not really
says i.

oh okay
says doc.

and then he sends me to this lady.

this lady sits me down in a vinyl blue chair
behind a curtain
and she says this won't hurt you very much girl
and then she stabs a fucking needle into my arm
and i smile really hard at her so it won't hurt.

then she tells me:

if you start to feel faint at school
just sit down
and **put your head between your knees**
and close your eyes.

this makes me *very* nervous.

then dad is dropping me off at school
and i am getting out of the car
and there is a pin sticking out of my backpack
one of those class-election buttons from
school
those popular kids running for junior vice
president or secretary or treasurer but really nobody cares
about them.

this pin
this button
in my backpack
it scrapes
SCRAPES across my thigh
as i am getting out of the car and i feel this
very sharp pain and i say "ouch"
and then "bye dad"

bye honey.

as i am walking to my class i feel some
wet
on my leg so i go to the bathroom
where i am all alone
and i look into the mirror
and lift up my skirt and see the red
dripping all the way down to my ankle

i see the big red gash and
i kind of want to smile
but i don't.

at the arts festival

i feel something besides
extreme self hate
and extreme euphoria-

it is extreme indifference.

i am sitting alone with a million people
on a grassy hill

with sunshine and two goofs
doing yoyo tricks
trying to entertain me and millions billions trillions of others.

but i am so detached and isolated
from the rest of the world.

i feel like i am watching the whole scene on teevee.

and the laughter from the people around me
sounds like a laugh track from an audience so far away from here.

i can hardly feel the sunshine on my skin.

when things start getting better

at the arts festival
and i stop worrying about being with my family instead of kelsey or charlie or
or
or anyone
rod stewart or jewel
dammit anyone besides them

then:

hey. they aren't that bad.

and i am walking to sonic and i see my reflection
in one of the shining windows
and i notice that my hair looks real cute

when this random skinny plaid shirt guy says

hey aren't you in *paisley collection*

and my face melts into a goofy grin and i say

yeah

band practice is a place
full of whimsical oddities
silly circumstances
blithe characters

and it is always somewhere
that i want to be.

i want to be there
with these funny bones,
these sillies that always paint
smiles onto my face
no matter how bad i wish that they wouldn't.

i remember licking giant lollipops at band practice and
putting on fake tattoos leaning over somebody's kitchen sink.

i remember eating pizza slices quick so the drummer wouldn't get any and
playing with charlie's dog daisy until she almost had an epileptic seizure.

i remember watching eighties music videos with terrible special effects and
the first time that scot got the synth.

i remember playing for neighbors and parents.
i remember laughing at nothing and whispering *i love you* into microphones.

making silly putty imprints of the amplifiers and the euphoria of plucking one string on
the ukulele.

i never want anyone to take this away from me.

but i don't think that they understand.

the asian supermarket

is good clean family fun.

i get lost in there talking to kelsey
on my cellular phone.

and marveling at this culture
and the silly japanese cartoons.

so i take pictures of everything that strikes my fancy.
which is everything.

and i stock up on the one food i could live off of for the rest of my life:

edamame.

mmm oh mmm edamame.

and a cute asian drink to bring to school tomorrow

and my outlook seems positive enough, doesn't it?

i'm looking forward to tomorrow

i want to live until tomorrow

this makes me happy.
for now.

i feel famous sometimes
when people remember my name
though i've known them for years.

when someone thinks of me half as
often as i think of them.

when someone reaches out
to prove to me that i exist.

but i don't.

kelsey is **the one i call** when
something dramatic happens
and i want to spill
or when nothing at all is going on
and i want to see if there is anything
dramatic that she wants to spill.

rosemary is the one i call when
i haven't talked to her for a while
or when i want to see her more
or when i want a really really *really*
good laugh.

charlie is the one i call when
i want a good conversation
or when something has gone
terribly wrong and i desperately want
to avoid discussing it.

i go on **walks** to the love tunnel
the place down the way
where rosemary and i used to play
where we painted, graffitied and smiled one day
where charlie and i photographed, i lay
and i sigh
deep inside
and i cry
it subsides
and i get up
and get over
and i sit up
and walk over
walk home
all alone.

night falls
and i open my blinds

enchanting, isn't it?

rain falls
and i open my umbrella

delightful, isn't it?

i fall
down the rabbit hole
so far down
i just
keep

f
a
l
l
i
n
g

down
         down
                    down
and it's
so dark in here...

frightening, isn't it?

my life is slowly stopping

i have stopped practicing my violin

it sleeps abandoned in its cold dark case

my nimble fingers have become slow and heavy

i have stopped painting

and part of me is empty and lost

i barely listen to music

though my ears beg for it even in the dark of the night

and my throat dies to sing beloved lyrics

i don't go to class every day now

i ditch with rosemary a lot

i barely eat anymore

and my stomach has become smaller and compact

so that usually after i take a few bites

i end up very, very sick

or maybe that is because i have started drinking so much.

i don't go out with friends anymore

i don't even ask to go out.

i never watch television

i never watch movies

i never sleep

which has made my face tired and old

and pale and sallow

i usually just stay cooped up in my room

writing poetry and thinking about killing myself

looking at myself in the mirror

and despising the reflection more and more each day

playing solitaire for hours on end

twisting and twisting that FUCKING rubik's cube

twisting it and twisting it until the tears come

and i cry and cry.

139

what's the point?

do you ever cry and not know why you're crying?
do you ever lie and not know why you're lying?

is this just another phase i'm going through?
is this just another hole in another shoe?

do you ever buy and not know why you're buying?
do you ever tie and not know why you're tying?

is this just another bed in another room?
is this just another corpse in another tomb?

do you ever sigh and not know why you're sighing?
do you ever die and not know why you're dying?
do you ever why and not know why you're whying?

what's the point?
what's the point?
what's the point of that point in the land?
yeah.
what's so grand about a mountain?
what's so grand about a fountain?
what's so grand about a lion and his roar?
what's so grand about an ocean and his shore?
what's so grand about an oyster and his pearl?
what's so grand about a boy and his girl?

what's the point?
what's the point?

do you ever sigh and not know why you're sighing?
do you ever die and not know why you're dying?
do you ever why and not know why you're whying?

what's the point?
what's the point?
what's the fucking point?

i don't wanna do my homework
i don't wanna go to school
i don't wanna brush my teeth
i don't wanna sleep
i don't wanna comb my hair
and i don't wanna eat.

i said i don't wanna go outside
i don't wanna stay in here
i don't wanna tell a lie
i don't wanna wake tomorrow
i don't wanna call a friend
and i don't wanna paint.

i don't even want to paint.

some days i'm not even attached to anything
i am always silent on the bus
i never talk at home
even in my dreams my tongue sits in my mouth motionless
even in my dreams i do not speak a word
i rarely talk to anyone about anything substantial at school
i rarely raise my hand in class
i rarely even turn in my homework
i do poorly on tests and it kills me inside because i
know that i am not trying and i think what
kills me worse than that is that i really really
TRULY do not care.

one little bit.

or maybe I do care because
in math class i get so upset
over the fact that i failed my test

so i cry down my face when nobody is looking
and i'm listening to my music
and i decide that i'm going to kill myself

so i get out my notebook and
i write a note to each person
that i care about

Letter No. 1

ROSEMARY DUFFY

you have been my escape when i needed one
you never were a bad influence
though sometimes i used that as an excuse in my mind.

you were loving
        understanding
        forgiving
        smart
        artistic
        talented
        beautiful

and oftentimes i considered you my best friend.

you made seventh grade the best time of my life
and i never forgot

Letter No. 2

CHARLIE JONES

you are the only perfect boy in the world.

it was my lifetime dream to be with you
still
after high school

to still hang out with you possibly live with you.

ever since you mentioned that trip to iceland
in biology class remember?
you said at the end of high school you wanted to take one person
to iceland to randomly say pack your bags i've got the tickets
i wanted nothing more than to be that friend that you took with you.

you introduced me to music books movies
that kept me alive under many circumstances
just a little bit longer
-it was *almost* enough.

i know you'll go far in whatever you choose to do
music art photography movies anything
because i think you're pretty good at them all

and i enjoyed every minute i spent with you
and there were so many things that i wanted to tell you

but i couldn't

Letter No. 3

KELSEY RENEE

i will never understand our relationship

neither will anyone else.

you and i went through a lot together but it
always felt a little lopsided to me.

our wants and needs were different
and though our love for each other was strong-
we disagreed on many things.

i won't forget anything.

good
bad
beautiful

you were the only person who knew certain things
about me- but don't think for a second that you knew it all

i love you

Letter No. 4

WAYNE MAYNARD

do you know

do you even know
oh yeah.

you probably do.

before the word slides off my tongue
it's already slipping from yours we
are connected
you see.

you and me.

it's a fantasy
i get lost in
when i picture in my mind
all the times
all the jokes

and i can get lost
going from
one
to
the
other

oh brother.

i'm gonna miss you, boy.

i'm gonna miss from now until
forever.

i love you, boy.

but i don't have time right now
to tell you.
and isn't it sad
that
i won't have time to.

...never.

Letter No. 5

MOM

you just needed to cool off

       i didn't have any space
you didn't have any space

       oftentimes you were unpleasant
to me
when inside i was feeling unpleasant
and it made me feel *much* worse.

but i forgive you because i know
              that it was *ME*
       who made you feel unpleasant
in the first place.

i wish i could truly be as great as you think i am.

i want you to know that i tried.

i'm sorry

Letter No. 6

DAD

i sometimes needed my space

but since you were gone traveling
you wanted my space whenever
you got back

and i didn't feel up to it

i liked hearing your smart opinions sometimes
and oftentimes i didn't care about them at all

because i was selfish

you and mom meant well and i knew it
                                    i knew you loved me

                        i just didn't *get* it

you didn't let me live (in MY mind)
and i constantly felt like i was wasting my life
in my stupid house
with my grouchy family.

which is my problem.

none of that was your fault or mom's

i'm sorry

i love you both.
i loved you both.

Letter No. 7

BENJAMIN

you were the greatest little brother
that i could ever ask for

you made me laugh
            until i cried
                        and i love you

i'll never forget that summer
you know the one
when we had so much fun

yeah
there are things that only you and i share

just keep going
            i know you can

                        i love you

are those the only people i care about!!

i wonder after i have written No. 7
and by this time i am crying hard

but by some beautiful miracle not a soul in my math class
(they have no souls)
has turned around to look at me
not even kelsey

who is sitting right beside me

and i realize that i can't think of any one else to write a letter to

out of all the people i know.
that's it.

just.
just 7.

and the best song
this song called "submarine #3" by the *starlight mints* blesses my headphones
and flows into my ears and so many memories
OH MY GOD TOO MANY MEMORIES
are jumping my brain
i see dancing and laughing and crying and playing and sleeping and
every other -ing verb you could ever imagine
all to this song this one song and i think

this has got to be the happiest sound

in the entire world, this song.

this has got to be the happiest.

and i'm soooo sad. i'm so sad.

reading *prozac nation*
scares the shit out of me.

this girl is telling my story
out of her mouth.

it is a scary story.

i am broken.

self-portrait

i try to draw myself but it is gruesome

it was okay at first
but then it turned ugly
and angry
and scary
and sad.

i think i need help.

i think there's something very wrong.

maybe more wrong than i thought.

maybe *a lot* more wrong than i thought.

self-portrait

154

the feeling i get from
filling out **the therapist's checklist**

is something that i will never understand.

checking the box TROUBLE SLEEPING
and the box SUBSTANCE ABUSE

checking boxes for CONSTANT ANXIETY
and UNREASONABLE FEARS

then

checking beside the words SUICIDAL THOUGHTS
and
finally
HOPELESSNESS.

and after i check those little boxes,
it seems i understand everything.

the whole world makes sense.
just for a couple of minutes.

i am walking in the rain

just so that i can use my umbrella
i love umbrellas
more than almost anything.

i relish using umbrellas
i tingle when i hear that it is going to rain
i anticipate popping open that umbrella
and walking in the wet.

so i put on my converse
my worn since seventh grade
(such a good year)
converse
and my favorite hat
the hat that has been through it all
and my mother's vinyl raincoat.

i grab the umbrella
and walk outside

listening to folksy devendra banhart
and the rain making little spackly noises on my umbrella.
i balance on the curb and occasionally
clumsy feet splash into the puddle

when i see in the football field
(so many memories in the football field)
two geese
dancing in the rain and shaking their heads and
flapping their wings
and i smile and just stand there.

looking at those two silly geese hearing spackly rainy folksy when i turn around smiling to see

my mom in the big scary white car the headlights pointing at me
her hand motioning for me to get in
she yells from the window

      don't you listen to your *phone?*

i don't answer her
my smile is gone
my one smile in a week
those geese
God those silly-

      you could be struck by lightning!
      it's dangerous get in right now!

i get in and again i am sad
i am so very depressed because now it is over
and i'm trapped in that stuffy car
so i tell her

thanks for letting me out of the house for two seconds

and she gets mad
and i hide in the back room
watching cartoons
hiding under the covers
lights off
eating m&ms

for the next four lonely hours.

my mom opens
the door to the back room
and my eyes have **this glazed
look** that comes from watching too
many cartoons and eating too
many m&ms and just being too sad.

i have been hiding under
the covers and it is hot so my
legs are sweating but i just
don't feel like taking the covers
off of me so i leave them where they are.

and mom says

c'mon honey let's go to target.

i see my friend karny working there
which is kind of embarrassing. she
checks me into my dressing room
where i try on all of these lovely
dresses and pretend i will have
enough money to buy them.

i show them to my mom and immediately
she says

how much

and i look and each one is 20
dollars so she tells me to put them away.
but she keeps the one i like the least
because it is just plain black
in the basket.

and she keeps talking about

don't you have any money left it's a 20 dollar dress you know!!

so when we go to check out i pick up the
dress by the hanger and start walking to
put it away. mom holds her
hands up and says

no no! i'm going to buy it for you!

and this makes me very angry
so i just pretend not to hear her
and i go to put it away,
the whole time hearing her yell after me.
when i walk back to her she says

why did you do that
i was going to buy it for you!!

in a very exasperated tone

and i feel *so angry* so i just smile
and say

no
you weren't.
it's okay.

i guess now i should tell you about

this thing.

this thing that has been in my mind for so long.

the only thing that i can't help but lie about because it hurts too hard
to say it aloud

when they ask me

have you ever wanted to kill yourself

i always say yes
then they look disturbed and say do you have a plan
and i always pause
then i say

no i don't have a plan

but oh i do.

i do have a plan!!

i have always had a plan.

the plan

on tuesday night
i will lay out all the letters that i wrote so long ago
(in disturbingly organized preparation)
on the floor in a row
in front of my bed.
i will wait until that magic hour
when my mom is washing her face
my dad is asleep and my little brother is watching
stupid wrestling i hate wrestling on the teevee.
i will sneak into the dark kitchen and leave
the classical music blaring in my room.
i will grab the knife out of the wood block on the counter
and hear that slow and careful *shhhiinnk* as it slides into my control.
i will carry it back to my room and make sure that the cd is on
orpheus and the underworld and as i listen i'll smile i'll write so big on that blank purple wall

YOU DON'T KNOW ME

and i will wait until the second movement
when i'll STICK
that silver sword of courage
that gleaming blade of forgiveness
into my undeserving belly and i will
STICK it in again

and then i'll die
as the last note sounds
and *beautiful* orpheus...
he'll take me
under
with him.

and won't it be creepy when they come in and find my body and the third movement is blaring?
the can-can is blaring. the happy slappy can-can and my body on the bed.

i think about it too often

it is stuck

a skipping record

a never ending song

of skips and scratches

restarting itself

trying desperately to fix its mistake

but in the end it only makes the scratch bigger.

then bigger.

then *bigger.*

where it was once wet on my leg
from the class-election pin
it has now become a scar
a big ugly scar across my thigh

i don't know why but i like the way it
looks right there and every time
i see it
it reminds me that
it didn't hurt that bad:

only for a second.

and i pretty much imagined

that this whole "part one" thing would
freak out kelsey renee
when i handed it to her in algebra

saying

heya wanna read my book

and she said 'sure' all glad-like
but both of us knew inside
that she wasn't glad to read my book
she was probably scared silly
and i almost fainted right there
when my manuscript left my hands
and fell into hers.

i watched her closely out of the corner
of my eye as she read it.

i noted when she started crying
and i watched her eyes widen
and i saw her smile.

something inside me was saying

yes yes!! i am a good writer!! i've hooked her!!

but then i realized she was not crying over a good plot twist
or something like that. she was crying about my life.

this book is not fiction.

this book is my life.

and apparently it is sad and scary and sometimes it makes you smile.

what will my therapist think
when she reads this book???

i just plain do not know.

my daddy told me that i should never ever EVER!! tell
the therapist anything that wasn't true
because i could end up in the loony bin
even if i was just exaggerating or trying
to make things more interesting for her to sit and listen to.

and i don't think i would ever do that but i'm not sure.

so... i'm thinking what if

i show this thing to her and she decides that i'm absolutely
bonkers wacko
and makes me go live somewhere else???

what if
this is one of those things that you're
not supposed to tell anyone
just keep it inside

but if i keep it inside
i will die with it inside.

very soon.

and my daddy told me that if i wanted to kill myself
then i needed to tell that to the lady. i needed to tell her
the truth. but that might mean that i might not live with
them anymore for a while.

what do i want

what do i want

what do i want

to do???

oh God

this morning
i stepped on that picture of Jesus

that i got with kelsey at dollar general

and we both thought it was so funny.
and we laughed endless, endless on the windy drive home listening to the *dresden dolls*
mumbling jibberish on the parts where we didn't know the words.

but this morning i stepped on it somehow
and all the glass broke
and i felt horrible.

horrible.

because that can't be right.

i mean,

who steps on Jesus?

really.

and i had another panic attack
                    like i always do
          i fuckin' always do

and i cried and i screamed and i thought of the knife
                                        like i always do

                    and i turned on orpheus and the underworld
                            and i thought of the knife
                            of the *shhinnnk*   of the knife
                                                   of the knife
                                                   of the knife

                                        of the end of my life
and it sounded so nice and i cried and i cried
                    wish i could say oh i died and i died
                    it comes in bursts
                    it hurts in my
                    chest
                    the vomithurts
                    the disturbing knife in my head
                                        ch-ch-chop-chop-CHOPPING
                                        up my legs

          should that disturb me
                    it sounds *so* nice

and i thought of my fucking i hate them so much i'll show them with this parents what
would they say oh what have we done to make her go this way why did she do this to us
and dead me would laugh and she'd cackle and when push comes to shove when cut comes
to **slice** comes to CHOP i'm not that mother fucking nice and i don't care that it will hurt
because i'm not afraid i'm terrified screaming in my bed pulling out chunks of hair digging
nails into my skin i hate them i hate them the vomit hurts i should cut off my head like a
queen oh how funny! a sob turns to a cackle how funny how funny i should chop off my head
then they will all say how did she die and people will tell them she fuckin' chopped off her
own head and they'll feel a big pinch in the back of their livers when they see the truth in
their eyes and they know i am dead that i chopped off my head and i think of the knife
                                        and i think of the knife

          oh...how funny! somehow i can't stop laughing

167

Part Two

The Escape

part two

tuesday
is too much.

oh buddy.

ooooh boy.

i go to latin class

and sit in my desk.

oh
i know.

i breathe real slow
trying not to waste anybody else's
breath

oh
i know.

i am going to die soon.

i think

i am going to die tonight.

and something inside me
looks forward to it.
and something inside me
is twisting my intestines around,

trying to make letters out of them,
trying to spell the word

NO

i type **all this** up and print it out
and carry it around in my hands
thinking:

it's okay

it's okay

if you need to
you can show it to someone

because it's right here in your hands, baby.
it'll be so easy to get help.

i am not planning on showing someone.
well
maybe my therapist
because i am seeing her today.

but if i don't feel like telling her
then i just won't.

it's all planned out anyway.

i might as well get it over with.

dad is checking me out at 3 something
and it is only first block.

i have a long way to wait.
but i have lived this long already,

i can wait a few more hours to die.

i look up at kelsey
during latin class

and give her one of the strangest looks in the world.

i only know it is strange because
kelsey's face is like a mirror.

her expression matches mine
when it settles in her brain.

i just wait a moment
and then in her eyes i can see my pain

so i look away.

and i lay my head down on my desk
and try to hear the silence.

but the silence isn't there.

then miss maggie
says

CHELSEA MARIE

and hands me a little blue slip of paper
that makes my stomach eat itself up.

in scribbly handwriting it tells me
to go to the office.
i am checking out of school.

BUT IT IS ONLY FIRST BLOCK

       THE APPOINTMENT ISN'T YET
       THE APPOINTMENT ISN'T YET

and in the deep deep pit of my stomach i know
that something has gone terribly wrong.

i gather my things
and oh God i am so scared to death.

i start walking down the hallway
when i realize i have forgotten my purseFUCKFUCKFUCK

so i run back down
and take it from the girl tina
who sits beside me
and i feel
this grossgross acid leaking upwards
into my mouth

from someplace deep inside of my body

someplace that is not supposed to be leaking.

i try to swallow it but it stays there
hugging my tongue

then i see my dad just standing all the way down
at the end of the hallway
looking at me
just standing
and he didn't move towards me
he just stands

and the acid tells me
that something is not right.

something is not right.

because my daddy has
never never looked at me in that way before.

i say	**he says**
daddy what's wrong	come on
why are you looking at me like that	we're going home
why what's wrong	we're going home
what did i do daddy	you've been weird
(crycrycry)	you and kelsey have been weird
(crycry)	something's not right
but daddy	we're going home.

he takes me home
and i sit around

then he takes me in my room
and we get on my computer

and he says
what's this

and it is this-

this poem called

THE PLAN

maybe you remember it.

and just to feel the hurt that my daddy must have felt.
i feel so guilty

that i want to die even more.

i go to the therapist

and **with her searching eyes**

she asks me
after we were all alone
and my weeping mother
and my father with the deep red eyes

(deep red where they are supposed to be white)

had gone
we were all alone.

she asks me about my poetry.

i shows her my poetry.

she says

> oh chelsea.

> oh my goodness!
> this stuff is so good do you know you could *publish* this stuff you're like the
> next maya *ange*lo chelsea oh my goodness dear this is talent!

but as she goes on
her face gets grim then more grim
and her eyes dart from word to word
and the pages start flipping faster and faster
until she gets to the end

THE PLAN

after she reads that one
she looks down at her feet and kind of rolls her ankle around
once or twice then straightens the papers and puts them back into the blue folder.

> chelsea.

> have you ever heard of in-patient therapy?

she tells me all about it
and she keeps using the word

STRUCTURED

and it scares me a lot
so much in fact
that i can't listen to any of her other words

i am just waiting for

STRUCTURED

to happen again

then she brings in my

crying mom red-eyed daddy

and tells them about

STRUCTURED

and they cry some more and their eyes get redder.

she says

> i suggest
> you take her
> to the
> emergency room right away now.

we get in the car
to drive to the hospital.

to drive to the emergency room.

i am an emergency.
my crazy brain is an emergency.

i cry the moment i get in the car and the cry
hurts so hard
so much harder than it ever has before.

because
i am an emergency.

i cry so hard
that dad holds my hand
and his eyebrows furrow together
in concern in worry in angst in stress in sadness
and we hold hands and i cry and he drives me
to the emergency room.

i look out the window in agony
as i cry on the way
to the emergency room-
and as we pull up to a stoplight,
a woman in her car turns to look at me
and what she sees is wretched
and she is probably frightened
and she is probably sad

because what she sees is
a crying sopping soaking wet adolescent walking death she wants to die holding hands
        with daddy she cries her eyes are burnt red what's in her head, she sees:

an emergency.

i cry in the waiting room
where this cool guy in sandals
that i normally would appreciate
just looks at me

and my red face
and my black eyes
and my shattered frame

the way my shoulders hunch too far forward
and my face is stuck in this awful sneer
the acid is leaking out of my eyeballs
and onto people magazines and teevee guides.

they call me in
and i sit on a chair in a little room
where this lady with tacky highlights
takes my blood pressure and temperature and puts a little hospital bracelet on me that
        says my name
she asks me why i am here

and it dawns on me that

I HAVE TO TELL HER!

i sob some more and try to say suicide
and she writes down some stuff and asks me if i have a plan

and i have to tell her

and i try to say stab

my
self

in

stomach

and she writes some stuff down.

she takes me down a winding hallway
and we just keep taking **right turns**
and i wonder

how big *is* this place

and when we walk through the hallways
all the doors are open.

and you can look inside
see what's going on in other people's lives
other emergencies.

none of them are pleasant

some are too bloody

some are too quiet

some are too stressful

some are too confusing

but one
is too sad

i see an old man

skin and bones and thin old man hair on his legs that
are exposed
wearing a little hospital gown

he says something to the doctor
he closes his lips back together when i see him

and he looks at me and his eyes say so clearly

HELP

so i jerk my head down to the floor
and watch my toes
trying to forget him.

i get to my room

**room number
twenty two.**

i sit on the hospital bed
and a doctor comes in.

he says it again

why are you here?

i look down at the ground and tell him plainly.
my dad is sitting in the chair next to him and i see him look at me.
wondering from where those words are coming from.

the doctor asks to read my poetry but he just skims through it and says

mmhm.

then he says you're gonna have to put this on
throws me a hospital gown
and shuts the door.

my daddy is still in here with me.

i say
get out.

he says
no, just change...
i won't look.

he turns around and i say
dad i'm not changing with you in here.

he says
chelsea just do it please.

i start taking off my clothes
and the tears start rolling down my neck and then past
down all the way
to my stomach and i can't believe this
but i am naked
and my father isn't looking at me but still-

so i try to put the gown on
as fast as i can

and he says
are you done.

i say
NOOO!

then i have the gown on
and i pull it tight around me
so tight to make sure that it covers
all of me

and dad helps me tie it
in the back and i can't stop the crying.

another lady comes in

i am ashamed in my stupid gown sitting on the bed.

she looks at me and says that i make her sad

and i think:

great.

she brings me two hot blankets that cover pretty much all of me.

then my mom comes in

and the lady takes my blood.

and my mom holds my hand even though i really don't want her to.

how i hate it when they take my blood!

i want to be the only one to take my blood!

and what the hell do *they* need it for!

i cry again.

that's when she says

someone will be back shortly.

a crazy woman

with wild hair and plaid pants
walks into the room

and peers at me through her plastic framed glasses.

i think

i bet she thinks she looks real eccentric.

and that makes me angry.
i don't know why.

she makes my parents leave, and i talk to her about this.
about that.
she runs through a checklist

she says what day is it
            what month is it
            what year is it
            where are you
            who are you
then
            why are you here

deciphering
that i have problems with
suicide and mary jane and peer pressure and booze and depression

but the way she looks at me
she makes me feel like there is nothing wrong with me
like i am just whining because my nose is running
or something

and she says

so you haven't really told me much
i guess i'll go make some calls.

i'll be back

shortly.

the wild woman comes back
and says

> you're gonna have to tell me more

i say

> like what?!
> what do you want to know?!

she says

> so what are you here for

i say

> i'm trying to kill myself!
> i want to kill myself!

she says

> oh. i need to go make some phone calls.

she comes back and i have a room at a mental hospital
and a man will be by

shortly

to drive me there.

we have been here three hours

or four

and now it has been five hours

and my dad has finally turned on the teevee

so that

maybe he won't hear me crying

and i won't notice that his eyes were red

and i will be too distracted to notice that my mom has started pacing the room

back
and
forth
and
back
and
forth
and
back-

i watch an old silent movie
about abraham lincoln and stuff like that
but i am not really paying attention.

then a really sincere fat guy walks in.
it has been so long!

imagine it!

in one little silent hospital room for five hours!

so his fat sincere face seems so nice
even when he says

       i'm here to drive her to the hospital
(looking at me)
      they told you it would be fifty dollars, right?

my dad is going to follow us **to the hospital**
my little brother is at home
at a friend's house
trying to explain why he needs to stay with them at midnight
my mom is going to ride with me

we get in
and he makes me sit in the front seat,
that sincere-faced fat man does.

and he is very nice about helping me with my seat belt
and making sure the air conditioner vent isn't pointing right in my eyes.

my mom sits in the back of the ambulance with a tall skinny guy
who keeps playing with his noisy cell phone and trying to make small talk

keeps asking sincere guy if he knows where he is going
keeps asking mom questions.

i cry as i look out the window
and wonder if i will live through this.

i want to smash my head through the window and
cut my face into a million slithers of red string

i want to punch out the sincere guy so that he
will crash the car and we will all die

i want to open my door and jump out into the busy road

i want anything.

but most of all
i want there to be nothing.

especially when i see the sign
the big white sign
that has the words MENTAL HOSPITAL
in blue
and they look WAY *too big*.

i want to cover them up, isn't this supposed to be a secret?
why are they so BIG?

oh God he's unbuckling my seat belt.
oh *boy*.

i hop out and my mom
like a magnet
stuck to me.

the sincere guy walks me to the door
where they push one of those buttons
on one of those black boxes

and the lady says HELLO

and the skinny obnoxious guy says WE'VE GOT A PATIENT FOR YOU

and she says OKAY WE'RE OPENING THE DOORS

the skinny obnoxious guy opens the doors and we sit in another waiting room
with more *people* magazines and teevee guides
to cry all over

and Jesus i am so afraid of this place already.

oh goodness what have i done
i shoulda kept my big mouth closed
and just killed myself tonight
like i had planned

then it halfway hits me
buzzes past my ear
barely misses me

the thought that
if i wasn't here right now

i wouldn't be here right now.

and whoa.

i still wish.
i still *wish*.

then the obnoxious guy says YOU MIGHT WANNA SIT DOWN SOMETIMES THIS TAKES A WHILE
and the sincere guy politely looks away when i start to sob
into my mom's shoulder
and she starts to sob into my hair

everything is getting soggy-
i can't see much.

then another lady.
she takes me in and mom and dad.
the sincere fat guy and the obnoxious skinny guy say goodbye and leave.

the lady, she is blonde and kind of pretty,
leads us into a room with three little chairs and one big chair behind a desk.

we all take our positions
and the shit flies.

she asks **too many** questions
we fill out too many forms
i signs my name too many times
i cry too many tears

she takes too many minutes
my mom gives me too many looks
my dad breathes too many sighs
the clock makes too many ticks
my stomach makes too many groans

she takes two too many polaroid pictures of me
and damn! i can't believe it!

after all of this she thinks it'll be okay to take two polaroid pictures of me
with my black eyes full of acid
and my stomach ache and this hell
this is all hell

who would *ever* want a picture like that

what kind of bitch

then she makes me say goodbye to them

my parents
and i know deep inside
that i will never see them again.

my mom knows too.
because she is bawling
like me
and my ribs and my lungs
are shaking and rattling
and ready to snap crackle pop.

they both hug me too hard.

i can't believe it.

the sadness wears off real quick and it is anger that takes over.

THEY ARE LEAVING ME HERE!
THEY ARE LEAVING ME HERE!

the woman only looks
a

LITTLE

sympathetic
and suddenly to me she is not pretty
she is hideous
resembling a witch
an awful witch

and her hair is awful dark in this hallway.
i doubt it was ever blonde.

she leads me down and down
and through doors that are big and blue
doors that she has to swipe little barcodes across
so they will beep and let her in.

she leads me into a place
that is spacious and light blue
and quiet except for the rap music
playing in the hallway.

there are so many florescent lights.
they sear into my eyes that are red
and burning already.

i don't care that i am going blind.

what is a dead person going to do with eyesight, anyway?

the witch takes off my necklace

and makes me take the lace out of my vest.

she takes my headband
and my shoelaces

my ring
and my pencil.

and she leads me to a big white room.

this is the quiet room.

she makes me take off lots of my clothes
so she can see if i have been cutting myself.

she doesn't see the big scar on my leg,
because she doesn't make me take off my skirt.

it is humiliating
it is so so sad.

i have to sit in a chair in this big room
and there are people

sitting in a row
at a long table

and there is one bed in the middle of the room
that all the florescent lights seem to point to
and i cry about that too.

a lady comes and takes my blood pressure and temperature
then points to the bed
under the spotlight.

GET SOME SLEEP.

i look up.
there are three people
staring at me

the florescent lights
are all still on
and burning my retinas.

the teevee is blaring behind me
i hate teevees.

the rap music down the hallway,

and the list of rules on the wall.
the clock.

i watch it tick.
for an hour.

then i really start to cry.
and the people at the table just watch me
and take notes.

i close my eyes.
i open them.

> *i'm still here oh God. i'm still in this* place.

lying in this bed

i think of

kelsey and rosemary and charlie.

they don't know where in hell i am.

nobody does.

i think of many things,
like the taste of tapioca pudding and
the feel of oysters down the throat.

i think of trying to break out of this place.

i think of the way charlie's hair curls around his glasses
and the way i always eat lunch in rosemary's art class.
i think of us all playing the marimbas and xylophones in the band room.
i think of the *starlight mints* and picasso.
i think of kelsey calling my dad, saying she thinks something
weird
is going on with me.

i think of when i first broke my arm and how i used to get excited about
climbing trees and reading stephen king books.

and then i open my eyes.

and *still* i am here.

i lay awake all night

alternating

one-two-three.

one-

look at list of rules on wall

two-

look at clock- count seconds

three-
close eyes

one-two-three.
one-two-three.

and there is this thing that bothers me.
number one and number thirteen are the same.

on the list of rules number one and number thirteen are the same.

they both say "no standing in doorways"
and i am worried that i am seeing things so
i read it over and over and over and over again
until i am sure
i am CERTAIN
that number one and number thirteen are the same.

then a woman walks by and i say
through a throat full of tears

"is it just me... or are number one and number thirteen the same?"
pointing a pale bony finger at the list of rules.

she shoots me a piercing look.

"maybe they just messed up. get some sleep."

i close my eyes.
i open them.
i read the list of rules again.

number one and number thirteen are the still the same.

it is the longest night

and i don't notice
between

one two and three

that the night staff has switched to the morning staff
and this **walrus man** is immediately before me staring into my soul.

he yells across the big empty room to the nurse's station

this 'un's already woke up.
need some uh her blood?

then a woman comes up to me
and she just gives off the most flustered vibrations
from yards away

she says

honey i'ma **just take summa your blood** sweetheart

and she grabs my arm and her long nails pierce the sides in a way that is just
        uncomfortable enough
to make me pull away.

she shoves something in my hand and tells me to
SQUEEZE THE BRAINS
and she lays my arm down flat
and sticks the needle inside.

it hurts worse than it is supposed to.

she looks concerned but
not in a sincere way
in a trying-not-to-laugh-way
because my vein is rolling around
and she can't stick the needle in and
when she tells me this i tell
her i am going to barf
everywhere so she says
ALMOST DONE
and then takes it out and
puts a big band around my arm and
leaves me in the middle of that room where

that walrus is staring at me
as he munches on a sandwich.

it is six thirty.
it is only six thirty.

goo goo g'joob

cut up sandpaper words spit out from underneath
rough thick broomy mustache
tips drooping down to frame two chins.
he leans back too far in his chair and i sit up in my bed
all black mascara and red eyes and white face
and swollen and sad and angry and
stupid and tired and hungry because last night when that
WITCH
asked me if i wanted any food i said no
even though i was *so* hungry.

where ya from, chelsea?

the City.

my voice sounds lonely and empty.

why are ya in this place?

i'm suicidal, sir.

oh. oh. oh. whatcha gonna go 'n do summen like that ferr? you seem like a smart girl.

i nod because i don't know what else in the hell to do.

what school juh go to?

millstone.

oh. oh. oh. good school?

yeah. i guess.

*oh. oh. oh. you know soh-ciety moves so fast nowdays, speshly for young girls like yerself.
        it wasn't no boyfriend deal was it?*

no, sir. no.

good. we see a lot of those. oh. oh. oh. we see lots of those.

then it is 7AM and **everything is different**.

i hear loud rap music blaring all of the sudden in the hallways.
i hear the screaming from bedrooms and the throwing of heavy furniture.
i hear toilets flushing in unison and a lady says

hurry up!!
make your bed then push it into room eleven!!

i get up guess you could say i got up though i'd never gone to sleep
really hurried and shaking and scared to
make my bed so quickly momma woulda been proud
then i push the bed
and my arms pop all the way down to my fingertips
in this little crackly way that is both creepy and pleasurable.

the bed is heavy and the wheels underneath it are awkward
and hard to control.

the morning staff just watches me as i bump my mattress
back and forth against the walls
all the way down the hallway to room eleven.

it is terrifying when girls start pouring out of the rooms
and their eyes are all swollen
and their arms are all bruised and cut
and their hair is all frizzy and crazy and unorganized
like raggedy ann yarn on the tippy tops of their heads
strands defying gravity shooting out straight as an arrow into the air.

they pour out of their rooms and give me a glance or two
but i am just crying.

i am just crying and crying.

i can't help it.
i can't stop.

all the girls start crowding around
this **one little mirror**
obviously made of plastic

(because it distorts your face in such an awful way)

but they crowd around it anyhow
to put on their makeup (waay to much)
or comb their hair
which will always look like loony hair no matter what they do to it.

some squirt it with water until it is soaked
but then it dries and is crazy again,
some try to gel it down with sticky goopy fingers
but a couple of pieces still stick out in the back.

i have no makeup.
i have no toothbrush.
this is my only outfit.

i watch them and i cry.

what are they primping for?

isn't this a *mental* institution?

after everyone is ready (for WHAT)
they sit down in desks around me still crying i watch them
and when they get too close to me my eyes get wider.

oh. i want nothing
to do with them and **it
isn't their fault.**

i notice two boys in the corner.
one looks at me from beneath
a greasy sticky clump of jet black hair,
the kind that might be clogging your shower drain
and he has the lightest blue irises and
the whites are so *pink*.

i shiver and look away.

stop looking at me stop looking at me please stop looking at me

every girl i look at smiles warmly back and i only cry at them.
a lady sits at the long table and says READY KIDS
and then starts listing names

it works this way:

she lists a name
she asks
how are you feeling today and what is your goal?
then she writes down what you say on a chart
then she does it again.
i quickly noticed a pattern:

deborah.
how are you feeling and what is your goal?
        i feel *great,* and my goal is to have a positive shift.
how are you going to do that?
        by following staff direction.

irma.
how are you feeling and what is your goal?
        i feel happy, and my goal is to have a positive shift.
how are you going to do that?
        by following staff direction.

morgan.
how are you feeling and what is your goal?
        i feel good, and my goal is to have a positive shift.

it continues this way through each kid, and something about the whole thing strikes fear
        into me in such a way that when i hear her say my name:

chelsea.
how are you feeling and what is your goal?

i cry and say

      scared. i'm scared.

nobody blinks. she writes something down and everybody gets up and leaves somewhere.
i get up to follow them, but a nurse pushes me back down into my seat.

you are on suicide precautions.
she says.
that means you stay right here.
and give me that pencil.
you are not allowed to have pencils, do you hear me?

some guy named mister jim
comes and **sits at the table and watches me cry**

then another man named terrance
comes and sits next to mister jim at the table and watches me cry

and i get so angry at them.

mister jim says
>   *you can turn on da tellyvision, and watch channel sixty nine.*
>   *da dee-scuv-ery channel.*

his voice is kind with a little jamaican rhythm to it.

terrance smiles with his eyes and says
>   *come here, chelsea.*
>   *come* here.

when he says the word HERE it is so much higher than
the rest of his sentence so

i walk slowly up to the long staff table
he looks at me
nervously swiveling around in his swively swivel chair
i look

scary.

i probably would scare myself.

i bet i already have crazy loony hair.
i can feel it.
i can feel the paleness of my skin with no makeup.
i can feel the anger in my red eyes.

he says
>   *why are you here chelsea?*
"suicidal"
>   *oh girl. you shouldn't ever wanna do that.*

I HATE THIS! I HATE HIM! WHY IS HE TELLING ME THIS! IS EVERYONE GOING TO TELL ME
>   THIS! I KNOW I KNOW I KNOW! I DO WANT TO DO IT! WHAT AM I SUPPOSED TO
>   DO! I HATE THIS!

>   *you should live yo life. you look like a real smart girl-*

WHY DOES EVERYONE *SAY* THAT TO ME?! WHAT MAKES ME LOOK SO SMART? MY FUCKING
>   *GLASSES*?! JESUS *CHRIST*! WHAT IS *WRONG* WITH THIS PLACE?!

>   *you should take advantage of them brains in yo head*

a big white-toothed smile is creeping into the left corner of his mouth

he asks me if i want a side hug.
i don't answer him because i am crying.
he thinks it is sadness or progress or maybe even a breakthrough realization.
it is anger.
i think he is such a dumbass.

he gets up out of his swivel chair

and gives me a stupid side hug.

as i sit in my desk the nurse comes up to me
and throws a big fat packet onto my lap and hands me a pencil.

here. work on this until group.
and you better be careful with that pencil.

i look at the clock.
there are five hours until group.

the front of the packet says this:

ADOLESCENT INPATIENT SERVICES MANUAL

and the first page starts out like this:

Dear Patient:

Welcome to our Mental Health campus and the Adolescent Inpatient
Unit. This booklet is your guide to the program. Please read it
carefully. If you have any questions, please ask a staff member.

During your stay here we develop, with you, a treatment plan which will
include the problems you and your family have noted, and any others we may
identify. This treatment plan will include your treatment goals, and ways
you can achieve these goals in order that you might return home or to an
appropriate placement as soon as possible. This plan will be evaluated and
updated weekly by your treatment team so your progress can be monitored.

i start to cry. this can't be real.
this can't be fucking real.
oh.

and the words start to smear and jump and crease and slide all around the off-white paper

Our program is designed to provide a safe and STRUCTURED environment to
deal with a variety of mental, emotional, and be h av ioral he alt h issue s. You
w ill be in vo lve d in a va r iet y o
                                        f
me n   i on a l   a
        t a   mo t   n d be h a v
          l   , e   i o r
                                                            al
        h ea l
              t h   i s s   u
                          e
                                              s

i set down the packet and let the tears come.
i just let them come out
and i try to avoid everything else.
i try to pretend that the packet didn't say STRUCTURED.
i try to reject this jarring reality and pretend i am somewhere nice.
i try to think of things like *vogue* magazines and *paisley collection* and painting with
turpentine and the taste of *hot tamales* and the calming sound of *the shins* and the witty
wisdom of kurt vonnegut
but nothing is coming.

it is all faded in my memory.

i know for a fact that i used to love these things a great deal but right now
i can't remember why.

i can't remember why.

i lay my head down on my desk and cry so hard
that my shoulders shake up and down and i kind of start to wail.

inwardly.

it hurts so much to cry.

i am all alone
except for of course the STAFF
sitting there

watching.

then i see a young girl.
right across the room.
she looks up.
she is hispanic.
she is hefty.
she has very short hair done that one way that i hate
where it's long and greased down in the front and
SPIKED
in the back but i don't really care because
she smiles at me so nice
and she is shuffling cards and holding a little chapter book
and she is walking towards me now.

and she is sitting at my desk with me now.

and now she is telling me:

look.
the first three days here really suck.
sorry about that.

215

she looks down at her hands
bitten nails
red fingertips
shuffles her cards.

a little smile tickles the corners of her lips and out comes-

> my name is jackie. you wanna know why i'm in here i'm in here because i
> just had a baby and my foster mom took her away so now i have post-partum
> depression. know what post-partum means? means you get all depressed and
> stuff after you just lost your baby. plus, the other day i pretty much tried to
> kill my little sister and that scared me a little bit so i put myself in here. i
> mean how bad would you feel if you killed your kid sister right? sheesh.

she is still looking down.
she shuffles once more and exhales then
dares to meet my eyes.

> what's your name?

chelsea.

> why are *you* in here?

suicide.

> attempt or just thinking?

well, it was almost attempt.

> you had a plan?

yeah.

> dad found out?

yeah.

> hmph.

she shuffled once more.

> know how to play california speed?

i wipe away a tear.

no.

> okay... i'll teach you.

we play california speed
and once i know the rules
i beat her every time
but she just keeps playing me
until they take her away.

after jackie is gone
i watch channel sixty nine for a little while
-discovery channel-
and i think about dying for a little while
then they come in with a tray for me
and i see a teenaged girl in the corner.

i remember her from last night.

she is big.
she is hairy.
she is morgan.

her eyes are gorgeous but her face is
masculine and large and sad.

she talks out loud about ridiculous things
like magical creatures and secret passageways
but when i turn around to look at her
her eyes dart away and she closes her mouth tight.

my breakfast is a bowl of cereal
and a carton of milk.

i eat it in three seconds flat so hungry from the night before.

they don't let morgan have a spoon.

she is wearing a hospital gown.

she is scaring me to death.

when morgan finishes her breakfast, she gets up
and sits in the very corner of the day room
underneath a blue chair
and starts talking
wrapping her arms around herself
rocking back and forth she talks and talks.

i under*stand*.
i understand morgan.

all the other kids get to go outside
except for me and morgan.

we sit and sit
and then there is a commotion
when a very masculine athletic black girl
is rushed inside
held up by two orderlies
and hurries into the doctor's office on unit.

she then rolls out in a wheelchair
with a smile on her face.

this thing is cool

she says.

i sit some more

and they take my blood pressure again

and i cry some more

then a nice lady comes in and tries to talk to me

but it is the same old bullshit so i won't waste your time

explaining it to you here.

                when she is done i felt that

                            false sense of comfort that i always

                                    feel after therapy.

then i sit some more and cry some more

and watch morgan do

the same thing.

they bring me lunch

and it is fake cheese on a bun.

i try to eat some but it is just too gross.
i am afraid to throw up.
i have always been afraid to throw up.

so i just don't eat lunch.
no big deal.

the whole day is full of sitting crying
drying up
occasionally having to talk to STAFF
watching the discovery channel
playing california speed with jackie
in between her therapy sessions.

i learn that she is naming her baby girl
neveah.

that's heaven spelled backwards.

the trashiness of it
makes it so beautiful to me.

the girl in the wheelchair
is full of attitude
a lot of attitude to keep cooped up
on the unit with two glum girls
like morgan and i.

she rolls around in her wheelchair
smiling a brilliant smile
and all of staff is captivated with
her energy.

she says
look here, morgan,
i can pop a wheelie in this thing!

and she does!
and we are delighted.

she learns to maneuver it flawlessly
and she becomes very independent,
doing things
i never knew
a person on wheels
could ever do.

then it is group therapy time
so terrance
tells all the kids to go to **the**
group room
which is a big cold dungeon
with a teevee and some black
leather couches full of foam.

we sit there and i look around
at all the kids and meet them
and learn their names
and understand them in a way
that i never would understand them
if i wasn't sitting here in a mental institution
looking at them and trying to understand them.

they all seem so strange.
they all seem so young.
they all seem so innocent.
they all seem so fucking *crazy*.

after group therapy
which was a movie
with some cheesy fat ass psychologist slash comedian
who visits kids at schools and talks to them
about racism,

we all go into the day room and sit.

some crowd around the radio that is on that boy's lap
(the boy with the shower drain hair, the blue pink eyeballs)

some crowd around the discovery channel
channel number sixty nine

most are playing cards
california speed
texas hold 'em
spades
slapjack
egyptian war

anything you could imagine.

the boy with the shower drain hair is
looking at me and motioning for me to come over to him

when THANK YOU GOD

the fire alarm goes off and it is mass chaos
all the paranoia-complex kids are freaking out
running around
saying they are going to be burned
alive in this place in this hellhole

the STAFF looks afraid and stressed and
rushes us all out and i am thinking ah yes the sun

but my eyes are black and beady

so it doesn't feel so good.

they tell us

YOU KIDS BETTER NOT STEP IN THAT MUD

and i look around

there is no mud.
there is no mud at all.

as we are lined up along a fence
a pretty girl i saw putting on dark red lipstick this morning

pokes me on the shoulder blade.

when i turn around
i am embarrassed that she is looking at me.
i still am not used to looking bad.
i am not used to people seeing me like this.

> who're you?

she asks me plain and simple.

> i'm chelsea.

> oh... hey.

> hey.

then we walk back inside the ward and
shower drain boy walks beside me and pushes me nonchalantly
so i will look up into his nasty eyes.

i do.

and he says

> so you tried to commit suicide so you could get in here?

i don't know what to do so
i sort of half-nodded.

he says

> yeah me too.
> i committed myself, so i can leave when i want to, but hey.
> it's food, right?

he laughs.

i start to cry.

we all go back into the day room
and they get to go back into their rooms.
i am jealous that i don't have a room.

my nurse eyes for me to stay here.
in my stupid blue desk.

a lady breathing hard
enters the room dramatically by tripping on her own feet a little
then catching herself but still blushing.

she walks up to me
introducing herself as my personal dietician.

               i understand that you are a vegetarian-

     yes. i am.

               so you eat no meat.

     yes. i mean, yes, i eat no meat.

               eggs? dairy?

scratching on a legal pad, then itching the side of her nose
i think, if i wasn't sitting here i bet she would pick it-

     yes. i eat eggs and dairy.

               fish?
    no. no.

               tofu or other meat substitutes?

     yes.

               alright. have you been eating the food we've been sending you?

     yes.
i lie.

               has it been alright?

     yes.
i lie.

               good. well, i guess that's about it. tell me if you have any questions
or complaints.

     thanks.

she huffs away
carefully watching her feet
desperate to exit the room gracefully
but fully knowing that i will always
remember her as that big fat lady who tripped.

and she is right.

i sit alone in the day room
watching terrance fail miserably at imitating
stevie wonder
whose voice is floating from the stereo.

together we listen to his greatest hits
and alone I cry in my little desk.

morgan sits across the room in her corner
though terrance keeps telling her
to get up and sit in a chair.

i think staff is afraid of her.

how sad. i mean, what a sad, sad thing.

now they are bringing me my dinner

and i can't eat much of it.

the food is awful.

it serves no purpose but

to remind me that i am living in

a hospital.

i want to say

and what's with this food

what *gives???*

but inside i don't really care.

i'm even thinking of purposely

throwing out all of my food.

refusing to eat entirely.

but....

it is the only thing here

that seems normal.

the only privilege i really own.

i am allowed to eat,

i am allowed short semi-supervised bathroom visits,

and i am allowed to cry.

mister jim says
you can go take your showa.
and he points to the door and tells me to grab
two towels and a washrag
and "they" will find me some soap.

all the other kids have personal hygiene kits.
fancy shampoos and body washes that
their mothers brought for them so long ago.

this is their home away from home.

i don't know if i feel left out to be without possessions
or if I am glad that i am only a visitor.

the unit bathroom

is a place that i have never entered before.

a beautiful black woman who works the night shift
named miss amy
tells me

        honey i'm gonna have to keep checkin' up on you since you're on suicide

ON SUICIDE.

what a horrible thing, i think as i take off my
grubby clothes and step into the shower.

it is so cold and there is no water pressure and
i use their soap and it smells so generic.

i step out and dry off and hear a knock at the door.

       you okay baby?

as it cracks open
i cover myself up quick
and hurriedly spit out

YES

then start to cry into the toilet
thinking i will throw up
for some reason i think i will throw up
and i want so badly to throw up because inside
everyone there is a child that believes once
they throw up all the bad stuff
they will simply feel better.

on suicide.

i hate that phrase. the staff uses it so casually.
so often. *on* suicide.

i've seen my file.
it's behind the nurse's desk on a big shelf.

it's a big fat black folder
and on the binding it says my name
and there is a huge neon green sticker
that says

SUICIDE

in black
so huge.

and every time i see that on there
i am so ashamed and embarrassed.

i am still in the shower getting dressed
when there is such a huge noise in the hall

and i hear screaming and fits
and crying and yelling and hysterics

so i just get dressed and sit on the toilet seat waiting.

waiting for it to **subside**.

because there is no fucking way i am
going to get hit in the head
with a desk thrown by some crazy person.

i am just not in the mood for that right now.

when i am done in the bathroom
and it has subsided in the hallway,
i go to sit in the day room
for a couple of minutes
and i play cards with jackie.

then someone on night staff tells me
to go and retrieve my bed from room eleven
and push it in here and would i like a **phone call**?

i ask who i am allowed to call.

he says your parents.

i say, no thanks. i'll just go to sleep.

but i can't.
i just sit in my bed and chew on my nails
until they are gone.
then i start chewing on my fingers.
i chew and i chew until there are little calluses from the chewing.

my hair still smells bad.
my clothes smell bad.
my bed smells bad.
this room smells bad.

i start crying again.
i sit up in my bed and i watch the clock.

i feel strands of my loony hair defying gravity.

sitting in this bed i remember a lot.

i remember this one time when
this random kid told me
he went to **my church**
though i didn't go very much
but he sometimes saw me
and he liked my band.

i was surprised to know
that he knew me
because i had never seen him
before in my entire life.

but sometimes we need that stuff to know that we are important.
sometimes *i* do.

i saw him at the battle of the bands.
i see him in the hallways.
i saw him at church once and sold him a *paisley collection* cd.
in the Lord's house.

i keep telling him i'll go to youth group but now
i'm in this place and there's nothing i can do.

i can't get out to go to youth group.
i can't get out to tell my asian friend tran happy birthday on cinco de mayo
and he probably doesn't even think that i remembered but in this
place that is all i can possibly think about it.

cinco de mayo and the forgotten youth group.

it is **another** sleepless night.

7AM again
and the rap music
the fucking USHER song
with that line
that annoying *yeah* that i will
forever associate with being crazy,
with being angry,
with really *really* wanting a drink.

just a sip.

i make my bed and roll it
into room eleven
and because they are watching me
i am constantly looking around
the
paranoia
is
so
unsettling
it feels like my eyes
are trying to spin
all the way around my head
to make sure there
isn't some crazy teenaged girl
creeping up on me from behind.

i go back into the day room
and sit in my desk.

staff tells me that today i will be seeing my doctor.
i am *not* thrilled.
they wonder why i am not thrilled.
i guess when most kids hear that they are thrilled.

i go to see my psychiatrist and her last name is **nuni**.
she is middle eastern and her accent makes
her funny.

but i just sit in that black leather chair and cry
when she asks me questions.

Jesus
one of the reasons i am in here
is because i never talk
i never spill my beans
i never just let it all out

that's when i think:

damn.
this is not going to be easy.

doctor nuni **says** she
isn't sure what my problem is

(WHY DON'T PEOPLE EVER KNOW
WHAT IS WRONG WITH ME)

but she is going to put me on some anti-depressants.

i'm not going to lie.

i am kind of excited to hear this.
i want *some* kind of drug
i want
to take
just *some*thing.

knowing that i am messed up enough to need a drug
makes me feel like i am in here for a reason.

but looking around this place...

at all these crazy girls...

i'm still not

quite

sure if i belong.

there's this girl
half black
half white
with glasses.

she bites her nails.
a nasty habit.
she also cuts herself.
a nasty habit.

she worships satan and many times a day
you can overhear her talking with other girls
on the unit

convincing them of his powers
his ways
his truth

and her greatest argument is this:

"i mean, if there was a God... why would we be in HERE?"

good point.

i go back into the day room
and play spades with jackie.

i beat her again and she
is starting to look really discouraged.

what kind of bitch ruthlessly beats a
depressive at cards?

i feel pretty bad when i see that it is actually
affecting her.

so from now on...

she wins.

then i go to my therapist.

murray.

i have never met him before.

he *looks* nice, though.

he is bald and he has big brown eyes.

his face is clean shaven

and he has the most relaxing voice.

his office is big and spacious

and he doesn't care if i put my feet

up on the big couch that i am sitting on.

when i am in here i can look out

the window and see the sun.

he lets me drink big cups of

SODA POP even though i am not

supposed to.

when i am talking to him

i can control my tears

i can stop crying for once

long enough to get some words out

and he says i am doing really great

and that he thinks the zoloft will help me

and that we will have family therapy tomorrow at eight.

he calls my mom now.

i panic.

i don't want to talk to my mom.

he puts her on speakerphone and tells

her everything we just talked about

then he lets me talk to her.

i ask her

WHERE ARE MY CLOTHES?

WHERE IS MY MAKEUP?

.

my **clothes** are at the front
and staff brings them to my unit
so that miss amy and i can look
through every single article and decide
what i am going to be able to wear.

there is something about clothes.
there is something to me about the way they feel.
the way they go together.
the textures.
the lengths.
the patterns.
the colors.

i am so afraid she is going to try and take that away.

first she makes me dump everything out on the floor.

she takes away all the scarves and my worn-since-seventh-grade converse because they
           have laces.
she takes the tights and the skirts because i won't "be needing them here."
she takes the paintbrush that my mom tucked into the side pocket and sticks it in SHARPS.
that makes no sense to me.
she takes away my favorite hat.
she takes away my camisoles.
she takes away all of my pajamas because the pants have drawstrings.

i pretty much have a couple of tee shirts, some jeans, flip flops, and underwear left.

i don't have the patterns textures colors.
i am in a hospital.

that doesn't matter here.

she makes me write **my initials** on every single thing i have.

this kills me.

it hurts so much.

because i KNOW

that later on in my life

i will be putting on this shirt

and i'll see the CM

and i'll *remember.*

after i have all of my stuff **initialed CM** with
that big fat black sharpie

miss amy gives me a basket to throw it all in.

this is your closet.
go put it in room eleven.

i put it in room eleven.

then i go into the day room.

there he is.

shower drain hair.
pink eyes
with the light blue parts staring, staring.

he has the radio on his lap
and he smiles at me
and **his face** is bright red.

the radio is playing that song by *the guess who*
"no sugar tonight in my coffee
no sugar tonight in my tea"

which i will forever associate
with his crazy pink eyes.

he asks

do you wanna play me?

holding out a deck of cards.

i know i know but i'm
scared he'll kill me
if i say no.

i have a feeling that in this place
if you just do what you're told they
let you out faster.

so in order to get along with this loony
i sit down at his desk

and try to keep my composure.

you a stoner?

he asks.

hmmm.

i say.

he keeps losing and losing
at cards

which makes me wonder
am i really that good at cards,
or is everyone in this place
just considerably stupider than i am?

i know why he keeps losing.
because he is looking into my eyes
instead of watching the cards.

why would *you* try to kill yourself?
he asks me in honest open bafflement

i say
just why anyone else would.
i fuckin hate my life.

oh?
what's so bad?

nothing really. nothing that you would get.
they tell me it's because i'm an *artist*.
i say sarcastically.
i over-exaggerate drama for artistic reasons.
i like to dwell on problems longer than others.
but really i'm just depressed. you know?

you don't deserve to ever feel that way.
you're a *pretty* girl.

a shiver runs down my spineEEW EEW EEW
oh God *gross*
then his knee touches mine underneath the desk
and i look up to see his eyes
and they are smiling at me.

one more game?

no thanks, bradley. no thanks.
i think i'm going to go to sleep.

you stoner.

(hmm.)

i gather up my poetry
(which i keep with me all the time)

under my pillow at night
the rest of the time
attached to my body
held close to my chest

and nobody says anything.

i take my bed out of room eleven
and roll it into the day room
where bradley is
still sitting there
by the teevee
radio in his lap mumbling
stoner stoner stoner
and shuffling those cards.

i lay down
on the mattress
and imagine-

my bed is rolling me all the way
out of this place...

finally the other patients go to bed
mister jim and miss amy
sit at the long table and watch me sleep.

watch me cry.
watch me sit.

i bite my nails some more.

i wish somebody would **hug** me.

7AM rap music
awake
and goals group how are you feeling
PERFECT I'M PERFECT!!
oh yeah then what is your goal
WHATEVER YOU WANT IT TO BE!!
that's right.
that's right.

the girl who tapped me on the shoulder blade
outside in the sun
says
hey.

hey. hey. hey. hey.

how are ya?

awful.

yeah. i figured.
it'll get better.

then, i can't help it. the curiosity is too strong.

why are you here?

she pulls back her sleeve and i see a big angry scar on her wrist

i slit my wrist.
she smiles.
my therapist put me on all these crazy drugs and i told him they didn't feel
right.
then all of the sudden i looked down and my wrist was bleeding like mad
and i had a knife in my hand. i told my mom.
she put me here.

just when i start to think she is a little normal, as normal as you can
be here,

she meows.

like a pussycat.

then she leaves
and jackie leaves
and bradley leaves
and morgan even leaves
and a bunch of other people i don't know yet leave.

the nurse tells me to stay.
i have **a doctor's appointment**.

when i walk to his office with the nurse i see that
he isn't a therapist.
he is an actual medical doctor.
he is big fat old, thinks he is much funnier than he really is.
kind of an asshole.

i sit on the chair.
and he leans it back
and a nurse sits in there and he says
so...

you're a drinker, eh?

i guess so.

what's your poison?

vodka.

how?

straight. shots. glasses full. thermoses.

hmm. very well.

he looks in my ear with that little light and then into my eyeballs.
the nurse smiles at something.

he says lay down
and then he pulls my shirt up
and touches my belly
in this way that makes me feel very very sick.
he kneads it
and he makes a little square with his fingers
and then he knocks on it in various places
and i want to yell at him WHAT THE FUCK IS YOUR PROBLEM

plus the whole time he is jabbering about how he used to be a drunk now he goes
to AA meetings and stuff but man in those *college* days...

he tells me how to mix certain drinks
he says you ever had a lemon something-or-other?
a raspberry this-or-that?

i look at him wild-eyed.

i guess i shouldn't give you any ideas.

he looks at the nurse.
she laughs.

we used to drink in all sorts of ways.
mixing it up with everything.
of course, if you're really brave...
(he looks at me)
you'll just drink it straight out of the freakin' bottle.

...right?

i go back into
the day room
feeling utterly violated

and a crazy looking short squatty black girl is sitting in my desk.

her nappy hair is shooting out in all directions.
her clothes are strictly wal-mart pastels:
baggy and shapeless.

she is wearing funny little house shoes with pink satin bows.

she has quite a mouth on her.

when i enter the room, she is cussing at the nurse.
she is yelling something about
ooooooooooooooooh i hate that muthafuckin miss AMY
i'ma muthafuckin cut huh THROAT

and her head is bobbing wildly side to side as she speaks
so charismatic
so energetic
so envious of her
i sit down silently in morgan's blue chair
and smile
for the first time.

on suicide
i have to sleep in the hallway
on my rolling bed
miss amy
is sitting right beside me
reading and writing and tapping her foot
to **that catchy rap music.**

i look down at my toes
and they start tapping.
t-t-tapping.
and i sit up slowly
wiping the mascara off my cheeks.
(i have been crying)
and i smile.

miss amy says
            you alright babygirl?
and i just smile
looking beyond her
where i have a perfect view into de-BOR-uh's room.

that song comes on.
you know the one.

"now i ain't sayin' she a gold digger..."

and i can see de-BOR-uh's short stubby silhouette against her window

and she is *dancing.*

my eyes are GLUED to her
i laugh out loud
and smile
and start dancing in my little rolling bed
shaking my greasy pale head all over the place
and throwing my white bony hands up
into the sterile hospital air.

de-BOR-uh hears me laughing
and turns around to see me dancing *with her*
smiling and dancing even crazier
bobbing and wobbling
wiggling and slicing shapes into the air
smiling so big with her little white teeth
and her eyes all closed up...

miss amy looks at me looking at de-BOR-uh
and she stands up slowly, smiling gently
and starts walking in rhythm
(in her snakeskin stillettos)
in the doorway of de-BOR-uh's room.
between us she dances
snapping her fingers
and her beautiful bald head
is smiling all over
and de-BOR-uh and i flourish with the attention

all three of us dance to that song.
you know the one.

until it is over
and i fall asleep
for once
ignoring the blood and sweat and mascara
all over my white bedsheets.

her name is **deborah toneisha.**

you say it de-BORE-uh.

not DEB-ruh.

de-BORE-uh.

and i learn real quick

what happens when you don't say it

the way de-BORE-uh thinks

it ought to be said.

she starts rolling around on the ground right in front of me
and yelling and screaming MUTHAFUCKA MUTHAFUCKA
and then all the sudden two more staff workers
are here and they are OH MY GOODNESS
WHAT ARE THEY DOING TO HER i feel my hand slowly creep
up to cover my mouth this is
horrifying.

they put her in "a hold".
that's what they call it.
and they stick her with two tranquilizers
right there in her arm
in the middle of the day room
right in front of my face as i cover my gaping mouth.

they carry her into the quiet room.
it isn't so quiet anymore.

now it is screaming MUTHAFUCKA MUTHAFUCKA!!

the quiet room screams
for a long time.
it won't quit
until the tranquilizer sets in i guess.

i sit in my own surprise
watching the discovery channel
and then i have to go to nuni.

this time i try not to cry
i remember how she wrote
TEARFUL on my chart last time
that indian bitch.

this
time
i won't let one tear escape from my body.

she says
how's the zoloft?

psh. i don't know.

well, it won't take effect for a coupla weeks.

oh-*kay*...

so...

so...

i think you'll be off suicide today.

hmm.

yeah, i think that'll be better. you can eat in the caff. you can have a room.

oh. good.

yeah. okay. we're done.

i go back into the day room and sit in my desk.
the kids come back.

we have a group therapy-
watch *king kong*.

very therapeutic.
i must say.

looking around this place
constantly critical
cynical
how can this be right?

how can **a place like this** ever be *right*?

back in the day room
they say kids go to your rooms
and i look at that nurse
who always pushes me back into my seat
and takes away my pencils
and she nods

room eleven.

i walk in slowly and see her.
jen.

she is so loud.
she is so obnoxious.
she is so the mother hen of this place.
how long has she *been* here anyway?

she says hi
and i look at the wall
where there is a scary dark poem written
and pictures of rock bands that i've always hated.

hi.

we start talking somehow and she's really nice.
but boy does she talk a lot.
and what she says just breaks your fucking heart.

she starts telling me about
her father.

he used to beat her
every single night.
he beat her so much.

but she says she always fought back.
and she never says
ONE NIGHT WHEN HE WAS BEATING ME...
she always says
ONE NIGHT WHEN WE GOT INTO IT...

she tells me about this one time
when he beat her up and he tied her to the ladder
of her bunk bed and put a dirty sock in her mouth.
he left her there for days and then her little brother who was
three at the time came running into the room and got
the scissors
and he was crying and he cut her out of that and he pulled the
slimy sock from her mouth
and she breathed and rubbed her wrists
and she hugged the little boy so hard.

we talk
well
SHE talks
like this **for what seems
like an hour**
and the whole time i keep my
hand glued to my heart
and little OH MY GODs keep escaping
from my mouth
but you can tell that
jen likes it
so i don't feel so bad.

then a girl named darlene that everyone calls "big D" comes in and says
JEN- CHELSEA HAS TO ROOM WITH ME NOW BECAUSE MISS AMY SAYS YOU'RE NOT
    ALLOWED TO HAVE ROOMATES AFTER *LAST TIME*!!

and something in my heart unexplainably sinks so low
and jen's face changes really fast and she looks over at me
and big D looks at her
and she says FUCKIN... DARLENE! GET THE FUCK OUT WE WERE FUCKIN TALKING!
but darlene stands in the doorway which is against the rules and now it is time for group.

we go to group and jen asks the group staff
why the fuck i am not allowed to stay in her fuckin room because we are
practically fuckin best friends.

the staff says i don't know.
ask your therapist.

jen crosses her arms
and pouts.
she says GET ME A FUCKIN GRIEVANCE AMY and then pouts.
biting her nails
picking her scabs
refusing to say a word to anyone for the rest of the therapy session.

when we go back in our room
and i am packing my stuff up to go next door with darlene
jen starts to bite her nails
and sits on her bed and watches me closely.

you're gonna fuckin hate it in there

she says between chomps of fingernail.

i know.

i say looking down at my slippers.

she's fuckin annoying and fat as hell.

yeah.

i say.

but i'll talk to nuni about it tomorrow.

okay.

i really will.

i believe you jen!

well. have a good fuckin night's sleep, then.

you too.

i go into big D's room
and she is standing up with her legs spread too far apart
looking awkward in the middle of the room
that **looks just like every other room** on the unit.

the white walls.
the two rolling beds.
the two desks.
the tiny closets.
the bathroom with no mirror.
the big black window with the morbid bars.

no doorknobs.
and when you sleep at night your eyes catch sight of things
you could swear weren't there in the morning.
writings on the wall by the bed that some bad-ass scratched with a secret
contraband pencil or something hidden away from SHARPS.

you see FUCK THIS PLACE
or WHY AM I HERE?

you see KILL ME KILL ME
scratched so small and helpless
and little tears drop from your ducts
as you think about the countless
adolescent girls who've blessed and cursed these smelly mattresses.

you see names scratched in and _____ WAS HERE's.
you see curse words and immature sexual drawings.

it is all there at night time
and in the morning you never remember to look
even though all night you remind yourself to.

it is such a strange feeling
laying there.
knowing more than i should
but still not knowing enough to ever satisfy.
wondering more than i should
but never wondering enough to kill me.

one night i practically bite through my tongue
because i am so angry and i have no other outlet so i just bite down.
hard.

and i taste blood
and i fall asleep smiling.

the next day it is swollen as hell
and i won't talk to anyone.

it is just the *place.*
i wish i could just accurately explain to you
THE PLACE.

de-BORE-uh has **this shirt** that she wants to wear.

and everyone in the whole muthafuckin hospital knows about it.

she starts yelling at every single nurse
that happens to walk by her desk

WHY CAIN'T I WAYUH MAH MUTHA*FUCKIN* SHIRT?!
MAH *MOMMA* BROUGHT ME THAT MUTHAFUCKIN SHIRT AN' *I* WANNA
MUTHAFUCKIN *WEAR* IT!

the one nurse who told me i was pretty
says
deborah.
stop wigglin your head all over the place.
okay?
stop it with the frigging attitude.
just calm down.

and de-BORE-uh says
AIGHT.
BUT I STILL WANT MUH SHIRT.

and the nurse says
okay
let's talk about this calmly.
like two normal people.

de-BORE-uh shlumps down in her seat.
OKAY.

you know what would happen to you
if you went out in your neighborhood
and talked to someone like that?

YUH.

what?

I'D GET MUTHAFUCKIN *SHOT.*

that's right.
or beat up, at least.

I WANT MUH SHIRT BECAUSE IT'S CUTE AND MAH MOMMA BROUGHT IT FO ME.
her head starts wiggling
MISS FUCKIN *AMY* SAID IT WAS TOO SHORT AND THEY WOULDN'T EVEN LET ME TRY IT *ON*!!!

the nurse says
okay.
okay!
calm down.

CAN I AT LEAST TRY ON THE SHIRT?!

maybe.

MAYBE?
MAAAAAYBE???

YOU MUTHAFUCKAS AIN'T EVEN *FAIR*! I JUST WANNA TRY ON MY *SHIRT*! YOU DIDN'T EVEN
LET ME TRY IT *ON* FIRST! JESUS! I JUST *WANT* THAT *SHIRT*!

terrance walks by.
de-BORE-uh has been at this for at least four hours.
he says as he kicks his swivel chair towards the long staff table,

this better be some amazing magical shirt cause you sure are makin a big fuss outta this.

IT *IS* A MAGICAL SHIRT!
*JAY-*ZUS!

the first time i see **my parents again**
i do not feel anger or spite or hurt
i just feel true love and relief and happiness
and things like that etcetera.

i hug them a lot and cry five-gallon buckets of happy
little glistening tears.

they hug me slowly and hard and they cry too.
well, mom does.

dad's whites just turn deep red.

but i know he means it as tears.
so it is okay.

family therapy goes by fast.
i just want to say everything right
so i can end up as far away as possible
from this place.

i just listen to the words but do not juice
them of their meanings, and therapy-automated
responses issue from my mouth involuntarily.

i say all the right things and they say all the right things
and murray my therapist says

i think everything is going in a very good direction
let's do this again soon

and then he says you guys can go to the caff for visitation.

visitation

we have to sit in the middle of the cafeteria
and this lady watches us talk to the people that birthed us
to make sure that nothing shady goes down.

i like watching de-BORE-uh talk to her mom
you can hear her across the cafe, that's what they call it here,
you say "CAFF"
de-BORE-uh is telling her mom
THEY STUCK ME RIGHT HURR IN MAH ORM WIFF TWO
MUTHAFUCKIN *NEEDLES*...

across the way
this little kid is playing cars
with his dad
and when his dad isn't looking the little
kid rolls the car back and forth back and forth
on the ground to get it all ready to let go
then he holds the wheels
and he sticks it on his dad's head
and it goes:
WHRRRRRR!!!

the wheels spin so fast
and it gets stuck in his dad's hair
he says FUUUCK
and the visitation lady says

      no sir.
      none of that.
      nooo sir.

murray walks me back to my ward.
you can go back to your room with darlene.

big D says
i'm **not used to** having a roommate you know.
i usually don't like it at all actually.

and her eye twitches really spastically and she hits herself in the head.
she keeps shifting all of her body fat from her left foot to her right
giving her the impression of a very nervous doughy slinky.
her brown hair is cut short.
spiky lesbian butch short
and she spikes it with ooey-gooey gel in the mornings.
she sits down at her desk where
there is an unfinished jigsaw puzzle.
i notice how big the pieces are.
i look at the box:
20 PIECES.

Jesus Christ.

         how long you been working on that? i say.

oh.
she says.
i dunno. three weeks or something.
i'm almost done though. i did a lot today.
see?

and her smile is so genuine even if it is not perfection.

i smile back at her
and sit down cross-legged on my bed.

look
she says.
i know you want to be with jen
but
well
how do i say this
she's annoying.

         oh.
         i like her a lot.
         i say.

she turns her head to look at me
and her eye twitches so i say no more.
she starts humming obnoxiously loud
and i am drawing a picture of a girl in someone's magazine.
(i snuck a pencil into our room shh don't tell)
she keeps humming louder and louder as if testing my limit.
i look up at her.

         ummm.

oh.
am i being too loud for you?
she asks.

       yeah.
       i say.
       sorry.

that's real good.
your drawing.
she says.

thanks.

it is time for lunch.

we get in line at the end of the hallway.
the boys have to stand in the back.
no mingling
say the nurses.
don't you boys even think about mingling, now.

they hand us our lunch cards one by one saying our names in disgust.
when i get mine i look at it.
it is yellow and everyone else's is white.

except for this one girl who is really fat and blonde
and maybe a little bit retarded
who wears purple lip gloss and it looks so terrible oh Lord.

i turn it over and so big it says **VEGETARIAN**
and i turn it back over real fast
trying to avoid a boring conversation with a crazy person.

but jen turns around sees the yellow.
she snatches my card from my hand and flips it over.
her eyes get a little bigger then they even out
and she looks up at me.

that's stupid
she says.

oh
i say.

she says
i'm not trying to be mean but that's stupid.

okay.

then the nurse tells jen to shut up and turn around
and i notice that jen walks really funny
why does she walk that way?

and we go through a lot of hallways
and the nurses swipe a lot of ID cards
under a lot of little laser beams
to open a lot of big heavy blue doors.

and then we enter the cafeteria.

it smells of lost socks
and macaroni
and the vinegar sweat of tired kids with no hope.

i sit by jen and de-BORE-uh and that girl who meows like a kitty cat.

i feel like i have **a little posse** because they all motion with their hands enthusiastically
and point to the seat in the middle of them all
and say
sit here sit here!!

it was alright.

i hated watching the maybe-retarded girl rhonda eat her noodles.
it was truly disgusting and after i saw it i couldn't eat another bite.
i'm sorry but you had to see it.
it was terrible.

de-BORE-uh started talking about how george dubya bush
is the muthafuckin anti-Christ children!!
i sway-uh to muthafuckin *God*.
i mean, he done urrything it *says* the anti-Christ done.

> holding up the holy bible
> this is what happens when
> you lock up a crack-head in a hospital
> and all you let her do is read the bible

she starts listing off all the things he "done" and i zone out
watching all of the noodles swim around
in the lake of saucy red saliva that is rhonda's mouth.

i cover my eyes and something inside gags me and
my stomach lurches like someone stepped on the brakes too fast.

jen says
you okay chels?

i say
yeah
but still i cover my face with my hands.

i feel a hand on my arm
and i hear:

> *me*ow.

on the way back from lunch
the gross, maybe-retarded rhonda
starts doing **this very weird thing**.

she holds her left arm up in a very awkward angle
and wiggles its fingers around spastically.
she then takes her right arm and saws it back and forth back and forth
in the air

she looks at me

I'M PLAYING THE VIOLIN!
she yells in my face.

her breath is rancid.

I'M PLAYING THE VIOLIN!

after lunch
we go back to the day room
and listen to **rap music**
and i feel my foot t-t-tapping
slowly my body starts to feel good
and i realize that i am humming the repetitive chorus
but i just push the thought aside in my mind.

no.
it's just because i haven't heard music in a while.
i don't really *like* it.
it's just there.

i sit by bradley and talk to him
for a little while then me and jackie and him
play a game of cards and i feel this very
awkward chemistry between them-
no.
not BETWEEN them because all of the
chemistry was flowing from *jackie*
and bradley was merely accepting it calmly.

it was grotesque (and sort of twisted in a way)
watching those two psychiatric patients trying
desperately to hook up in a mental hospital.
trying so hard to dodge the nurse's glance so they can touch hands-
maybe for only a second.

one day jackie comes back from "school" which is
held down the hallway in a little room.
i haven't been enrolled yet.
i don't wanna think about it.
but she comes back with this story typed out and
sits down between bradley and me
touching her fat legs provocatively,
exposed in little teensy shorts.

i read it and it is a story where the characters have no names.
they are simply "the girl" and "the boy".
occasionally they are "the lovers".
it is about two anonymous young people who fall in love
when they meet at a mental hospital. when they see each other
a second time at ANOTHER mental institution, they know that
it is meant to be.

it is truly awful writing, common words are spelled every which way and
the grammar is that of maybe a first grader. or an illiterate cocker spaniel.
but i give her a genuine fake smile and say
aww that's so sweet.
it's really good, jackie.

still feeling guilty for beating her in cards,
and watching the way bradley looks embarrassed when
he reads it slowly to himself.

the moral of her story?

crazy is as crazy does.

love?
desperation.
longing to belong.

fate?
returning conflict.
insanity.

from then on i watch how i talk to bradley
not wanting to overstep jackie's boundaries

which is fine with me
the kid freaks me the hell out.

it is my **laundry day** and right as i am putting
my clothes in the dryer i am called to talk with nuni
and then murray.

nuni just asks how it is hanging and i just lie to her
that things are splendid and she swallows it down
without a care.

murray and i talk and it feels good to talk
to murray because i like his office and i like
my secret SODA POP and i like the way he is.

this time he tells me to bring my poetry and i say fine.

i bring it
hold it tightly to my chest and the
little blue folder is falling apart
and the business card of a former therapist drops
from the ripping pocket.

he takes it in his hands and leans back in his chair and sighs
as if he is saying:

here we go.

and i have the exact same feeling.

he starts to read and says
i won't read the whole thing it's pretty long.

       then

hey some of this stuff is pretty cool!

       then

oh but i can see how this could freak out your parents.

occasionally he regurgitates my words back to me
muttering a chuckle or
a nodding in silent understanding

and just like with my other therapist, the pages
start to turn faster and faster and he just keeps reading
and reading even though he said he wasn't going to-

because it is good?
because i am crazy?
because?

and at the end
at THE PLAN he says

wow.

we talk about it for a little bit
mostly about how what i was doing
writing it down
is a very good way to therapeutically
release a lot of emotion.

i know.

and you should channel all of those
feelings in to create something besides
just self-loathing
and misery.

i know.

and by the way i think you're very very good
and you should keep writing. it's really coming
along nicely. it's very interesting.

i know.

the magical shirt

de-BORE-uh finally gets her shirt back
after filing grievances against all the nurses
and threatening everyone on the unit

she finally gets her shirt.

and she wears it to group.
she sits next to me
and she says
YOU LIKE MY SHIRT?
i say
yeah.
it's really cute.

it is just a normal pink shirt.

but... i have to hand it to her.
it is NOT too short.

i go back to the day room
not feeling really any better

actually a little worse from the
sudden jolt of carbonated caffeine
that just hit my empty tummy
but don't worry about me i'll be okay.

i sit with meowing girl and
her hair is wet because they've started showers
early today.
miss amy is here.
miss amy is very clean.

i say hey how are you

she says something to me in japanese.

i look away.

i see a little girl named nicky
watching teevee and laughing in the cutest way
but in two-second intervals
constant giggles.

i go sit between her and bradley
and bradley looks at me with his
heroin eyes and i say hey
what are you guys watchin'?

pee wee herman!
says little nicky
giggling maniacally.

oh i love him
i whisper
and scoot my chair closer
so i can hear
the rap music is up very loud
today.
miss amy likes rap music.

as i watch pee wee
i try to pretend that it doesn't remind me of the time i
watched it with rosemary painting on her bedroom floor
and she asked me if i wanted to smoke pot and i simply
said no thanks.

i try to pretend it doesn't remind me of charlie and his tim
burton enthusiasm.

i try to pretend it doesn't remind me of my dad always saying
i know you are but what am i.

i try to pretend it doesn't remind me of my cute little dog speck.

i try to pretend it doesn't remind me of chloe telling me
i'm soooooooooorrrry in her pee wee voice after she has
made me angry.

but it doesn't work.
i can't help it.

i think of it all.

i am enrolled into "school"
and the "teacher" is a really snooty bitchy skinny black woman
who looks pretty pissed off *all* of the time.

she says all the rules in one breath:
these are the rules no cursing keep your hands to yourself finish all your work no horseplay
no speaking unless spoken to no food no drinks no gum no pencils or pens unless i give them
to you no spiral notebooks no reading unless told to no cheating no communication of any
kind to any other students no whining no tattling pay attention no drawing no sleeping no...

and the list goes on and on and she is so monotonous that i yawn outloud very rudely.
we stand up for the pledge of allegiance and she gives them an assignment
and kids ask stupid questions and big D laughs.

i raise my hand and say "i don't have anything to do, ma'am."
she says oh yeah get up here you need to take your test.
i get up and she hands me a piece of paper
and says do as much as you can then give it back to me.

it is so simple that i finish 50 question in five minutes.
it is math and science and reading and spelling and other shit that i learned in third grade.
i finish it all and return it to her.
she says hmm very good now sit down right here.
i sit beside her and she gives me a piece of paper.
she says this is a spelling test write down the words i say.
yes ma'am.

the.
> T-H-E.

at.
> A-T.

him.
> H-I-M.

you.
> Y-O-U.

people.
> P-E-O-P-L-E.

school.
> S-C-H-O-O-L.

honest.
> H-O-N-E-S-T.

literature.
> L-I-T-E-R-A-T-U-R-E.

fraternal.
> F-R-A-T-E-R-N-A-L.

ambiguous.
> A-M-B-I-G-U-O-U-S.

monochromatic.
> M-O-N-O-C-H-R-O-M-A-T-I-C.

very good. what math class are you in at school?
algebra II, ma'am.
here.
she hands me a big book.
find where your class left off.

i get to my seat start flipping the pages
when nuni comes in:
"i need to speak with chelsea."

this is how it goes down

nuni: chelsea, i think we need to move up your dosage a little.

me: okay.

school is so easy.

i hate it.

it is the hugest waste of my time.

we watch movies.

we do "homework."

i always finish in two minutes flat

and the teacher just pretends not to notice.

i just sit and wait

for it to be over.

kinda like high school.
kinda like
back
home.

at visitation daddy looks across the table at me
while i sip some contraband soda pop

and he says:

honey.
if you EVER stop painting again like you did,
i'll know that **something is very wrong.**

the girl in the wheelchair
is rooming with satanic girl
and they stay up all night
talking about satan and tearing
apart the bible.

they talk about it at lunch
and satanic girl seems so
sweet outwardly but
inwardly i think something
may be tremendously wrong.

one night the girl in the wheelchair
gets sick and she rolls herself
into her bathroom and throws up
everywhere.

i can hear her sickness over the rap music.
i can hear it splashing into the toilet.
over
and
over
and
over.

she is not at school the next day.
she is not in group.
she is not in the cafeteria during meals.
she is not rolling around enchanting us with her smile and her wheels.
she is spewing all inside the rim of a porcelain bowl.

goals group

soon enough i start getting the hang of this:

deborah.
how are you feeling and what is your goal?
        i feel *great,* and my goal is to have a positive shift.
how are you going to do that?
        by following staff direction.

irma.
how are you feeling and what is your goal?
        i feel happy, and my goal is to have a positive shift.
how are you going to do that?
        by following staff direction.

amy.
how are you feeling and what is your goal?
        i feel good, and my goal is to have a positive shift.

chelsea.
how are you feeling and what is your goal?
        i feel good, and my goal is to have a positive shift.

just say it.
just say the words
just spit them out and they'll all leave you alone.

during one of miss amy's groups she says
come on kids it's time for group. hey! let's get in the horseshoe, **you kids like the horseshoe?**

yeah   yeah   yeah
                          yeah   yeah   yeah
        yeah   yeah   yeah   yeah
                                                    yeah

so we sit in the horseshoe
little blue desks forming a semicircle
and miss amy starts to talk about our ladybugs so the boys have to leave.
mister jim says JEEsus amy and taps the boys on the head so they can go watch teevee.
miss amy tells us girls all about our monthly ladybugs.
i know about all that. it's been taught to me but i understand that not all these girls know.

she starts to tell us how to take care of ourselves and her beautiful bald head and her
designer boots and her raw wool scarf all sink into my soul and i think "oh miss amy. oh
you are the greatest."
she tells us to buy ourselves flowers. don't wait for the boys. they don't know.

at this moment i look around at all these girls.
we have so much in common
there are thirteen of us and we are all sitting in little blue desks and we are broken.
we all have pale faces and slouching shoulders and scabby fingernails.
we all hate our parents.

i feel included.
so a PART of something
for the first time and instead of being excited it makes me sad.

i am pale and i am scabby and i am slouching and i am broken.
and that is why i belong.

after it is over i have to take my shower
and after my shower is over i have to
take my phone call and i decide to do that this time.

mister jim says
who you wanna call?
i say
my mom.

he dials the number and i sit
in the chair across from him.

he looks over at me and
tells me

i got the answering machine.
they ain't home.
sorry

and i wave my hand
it's fine

but if it's fine
why am i crying

if it's so fine
why does my heart hurt so bad

i say outloud
on my way to room twelve
they're probably just at benjamin's baseball game.
yeah that's probably just it.

but i am crying so hard anyway
and big D says
you alright?

and i don't answer her because what does she know.
what does she know.

i just bite on my fingers
and scratch marks on my arms
and cry a lot
and then have cruel lies of dreams
that i am back home.

the next morning there is terrance
and something about him is cruel
at 7AM when usher keeps saying yeah yeah yeah
from the stereo speakers in the hallway
and we get ready around the little mirror
and we go to the bathroom in our little toilets
and then terrance locks our rooms
and says

kids line up and getchur candy

so we all get up in line and take our meds.
one by one
the nurse calls our names
and gives us a little white paper cup full of pills
and we spill it into our mouths
and swallow with another little white paper cup
full of water.

then the nurse says ahhh
and you have to open up your mouth stick out your tongue
like a little baby so she can make sure you swallowed your pills.

your candy.

i *hate* terrance.

candy???
oh that bastard...

when i go up to the nurse's station to get my pills
the nurse says

you know **you are a very pretty young lady.**

i say pshhh.

and she says come here jim.
don't you think chelsea's a pretty girl?

jim says yes'm. very pretty girl.
and he winks at me and smiles
very nice.

i am not convinced
no ma'am
but i say thank you.

and she says

"say ahhh"

so i do.

and she makes sure i actually swallowed my

candy.

after we take our pills
terrance says
KIDS LINE UP
and we line up and we can tell
that it is raining because it feels
so comfortable inside like it always
feels when the clouds wring themselves out.

but we are lined up
and this is the first time i've been outside
since that god-awful fire alarm.

this time there is mud.

we try not to step in puddles
and little manic giggling nicky
giggles all the way to the gym
and her frizzy curly blonde little
**pigtails get sopping wet from the
misty sky.**

the gym
is really weird
and the meowing girl
who occasionally pulls
a little tiny book from her jeans' pocket
to look up words in japanese
is standing in the middle of the gym floor
wearing combat boots
and her eyeliner is smeared.

i say
so do you like...
play basketball and stuff?

she meows then looks around.
no.
i hate this place.

she pulls a huge fantasy paperback
with dragons and scripty text on the cover
from behind her back
and finds a corner to call her own.

i sit down by jen
and she is writing a letter and listening to the radio.
i cry when a *green day* song plays and wonder
what the hell is my problem.

kids are going haywire in here.
and the craziness echoes off of the padded walls.

there are little plastic boards with lots of wheels
underneath them
and even the really fat girl
gets a push-

there are loony versions of relay races
and there is a romantic one-on-one
basketball game going on over
there with jackie and bradley,
i notice.

oh jackie with her heaven spelled backwards.
oh bradley with his shower-drain hair.

what a marvelous couple!

i do hope they work out.
i can only imagine what their fat mexican heroin-addicted murderous children will look like.
what a marvelous couple.

i *say*.

then jen gets up to change the radio station
and this black girl with glasses says
I WAS FUCKIN LISTENING TO THAT
and jen gets all up in her face and says
WANNA GET INTO IT
and there is a girl leaning over by jen,
scratching her head
and her long brown hair is almost touching the ground.

her name is natalie
and she is fat and weird
and her "attitude problem" just makes her look real stupid
not badass like jen's or de-BORE-uh's.

jen looks
at her
scratching her head like that
and says FUCK NATALIE, STOP GETTING YOUR **FUCKIN LICE BUGS** ALL OVER ME
and natalie gets all heated up in this fat-little-bespectacled-white-girl kind of way
and says YOU'RE THE ONE WITH THE FUCKIN LICE BUGS and
jen throws a basketball and it goes right past natalie's face.
right past.

me and meowing girl
sit and watch this scene in silence.
she even puts down her fantasy paperback for a minute.

natalie starts to scream and yell and throws basketballs everyplace
and jen starts to laugh and terrance
has to put natalie in a hold and take her back on unit.

we all have to leave the gym now.

at goals group in the morning staff sometimes remembers to tell you what level you're on.

did i tell you about **the levels**?

this is how they work.

the orientation level:

- one ten minute phone call to family per day
- can attend school (whoopee!)
- can have free time (but can't use pencils, go in bedroom, use the bathroom unsupervised, listen to music, eat in the cafeteria, sleep unsupervised, earn points for privileges, go outside, or really do anything besides sit and cry all by themselves in a little desk... supervised, of course. all crying must be fucking supervised, naturally.)
- bedtime is 9 sunday friday through thursday, 9:30 on friday and saturday

level one:

- receive one ten minute phone call to family per day
- may eat in cafeteria with other crazy-ass patients
- attend school
- can attend outside or gym activities
- can have free time (still no freakin pencils)
- bedtime is 9 sunday through thursday, 9:30 on friday and saturday

level two:

- receive two ten minute phone calls to family per day, *and* two ten minute phone calls to friends or family per weekend
- may eat in cafeteria with other crazy-ass patients
- attend school
- can attend outside or gym activities
- can have free time
- bedtime is 9 sunday through thursday, 9:30 on friday and saturday
- may have two vouchers for snacks (otherwise, all the other kids get snacks and you sit and watch them eat)
- may lead community group
- may have off-unit passes with family or worker

level three:

- receive two fifteen minute phone calls to family or friends per day, *and* three fifteen minute phone calls to friends or family per weekend
- may eat in cafeteria with other crazy-ass patients
- attend school
- can attend outside or gym activities
- can have free time
- bedtime is 9 sunday through thursday, 9:30 on friday and saturday
- may sleep in one hour later on saturdays and sundays (all the way to eight o'clock in the morning!)
- may lead the lunch line with other level threes
- may have access to the big radio on unit (if it's not sitting in bradley's greasy lap)
- may have two vouchers for snacks twice during the week
- may lead community group
- may have off-unit passes with family or worker

and you get points according to how you act each day.

guess how i get to level three my first day after orientation?

i just sit there every day and keep my mouth shut.
i just sit there and shut up
unless they tell me to say something

then

i say *exactly* what they want to hear.

but
later
at night
i cry about it
very hard.

de-BORE-uh is restricted on unit
for threatening staff

again.

when we go back to the day room
i see her sitting in her desk and she waves at me.
i wave back she says HAAAY GUURL.
and i smile wide.

she says
YO WHAT'S YOUR FAVORITE COLORS?
i say **well i like purple and i like green**.
so she says
AIGHT and starts coloring hard on
some sheet she got from staff.

purple and green.

YOU LIKE ORANGE GURL?

yeah.

KAY.

then she goes back to coloring
as we watch *barber shop* around the teevee
and listen to some nice good rap music.

is my hair sticking up?
oh well.

miss amy says in group that the little boy who never talks is **a little devil at night**.

he screams and he yells and he cusses and he thrashes and he threatens.

i wonder to myself how i could have never heard him before.

is that why the rap music is turned up so loud?

the little boy who is so sweet and quiet during the day is such a little devil in the nighttime.

art class, fart class
the pretty nurse with blonde hair (i *think*)
takes us through the blue doors
to the caff
where we all take our seats at the longest table.

in front of each of us is
a piece of white stock board
a little box of multi-purpose colored pastels
and a worksheet with little faces all over it

there's a smily face and under that one it says HAPPY
there's a frowny face and under that one it says SAD
they even go as far to illustrate ANXIOUS, FRIGHTENED, SILLY, BORED, and LOVESTRUCK

blondie tells us our instructions:

okay kids. i want you all to draw an emotion on that piece of paper... *buuuut*... i DON'T
(her eyebrows raise at this point) want you to draw any faces or any words.

all the kids look around at each other as if to say "sheesh."

i am smushed between maybe retarded rhonda
and the meowing pseudo-jap

who both reach for their little box of pastels.

i look at my piece of paper
and it looks blanker than
anything i've ever seen in my life.
almost blank enough that i couldn't ever
fill it up.

like me?

i picked up the purple
and swirled it across the paper
creating twistiness like smoke from a cigarette
like the tip of a rat's tail
like the teardrops that make random little trails down your cheeks.

i add in orange and green
busily smudging away my fingertips
and mixing in unplanned tears
that fall from my face.

oh, ART.
ohhh...

i'm not inspired, per se, but i'm a very happy camper.

a black lady comes up and says wow
i nevuh seen designs like those befoh.

and i just smudge some more.

when i am done i give it to the blonde nurse and she says
very VERY VEEERRYY good job, chelsea.
i'm so impressed
but...
what emotion is this expressing?

i look away and as i walk away i mumble over my shoulder:

"horror."

we have a group therapy with miss amy
and she's always fun don't you guys think so?

well we all sit in the dungeon
and she asks each of us our birthdays
and she rips out pages from one of those little calendars
that have fashion tips one for each day

she says with her black bald head
and her chocolate skin
and her snakeskin stilettos
and her cashmere sweater
"okay kids." and we all silently read our birthday
fashion tips to ourselves
and the two boys blush at theirs.

miss amy says this group is about stress
we are going to go around the room and read our fashion tips
and jen stops biting her fingernails and says
but what the fuck does that have to do with-
and miss amy says now jen
please read your card we'll start with you.

jen glares at miss amy
at her black bald head
and her chocolate skin
and her snakeskin stilettos
and her cashmere sweater

"try wearing a great scarf with any 'blah' outfit.
a colorful scarf is a great and easy way to play up simple classics."

and jen looks up from her card and smiles.
we go around the room
smiling at everyone else's fashion tips
stuttering and blundering as we read our own.

we all laugh when bradley starts to read his out loud
then blushed and stops.
he looks up slowly then walks up to miss amy,
hands her his card.

she raises a skinny black eyebrow at him
and he goes back to his seat.
she looks down at his card.
"oh Lord bradley." she chuckles.
it is a charming thing.
her chuckle is a sparkling, charming thing.
"oh Lord bradley i'm sorry baby."
she looks back down at the card and reads it aloud:

"many women do not know how to accurately find their correct bra size..."
she starts.
we all start laughing
cracking up and de-BORE-uh has her hand over her mouth
and little *puh-puh-puh*s are coming out of it
and i am holding my tummy cause i think i might blow chunks
and little nicky is about to pee in her pants
and big D is jiggling around all over the couch like jell-o
and miss amy is chuckling, charming, sparkling
and the two boys are looking around, smiling, blushing
and even jen stops biting her nails to laugh out loud (a big HAH HAH HAH)
so we can all see her horsey teeth
and we all love it.

we all love it.

after the fashion group we are all laughing and smiling
and everyone is in a good mood which is really saying something
when you are in the company of a bunch of psychopaths and suicidals.

miss amy says
now remember how i said that this group was about stress?
jen says
yeah. psh. it wasn't.
and she looks around the room
smirking as if to say "am i right?"

and miss amy says
that's where you're wrong.
her eyes twinkle in this
absolutely enchanting way.
jen shrugs and bites her nails.

miss amy looks around at all of us and says
isn't it different to not talk about drug abuse and racism
and attitude adjustments and negative thinking and to just
talk about something silly like scarves?

there are nods and smiles all around.

satan girl says
and i hate that damn fat psychologist guy.

everyone laughs.

and de-BORE-uh yells
i love that fat muthafucka!

we crack up.

miss amy says
shhhhhh.
listen to that.

we listen.

what do you hear?
                  white noise.   nothing.   silence.
   nothing.   peace.
              the buzzing of the lights.   calmness.
quiet.

exactly, kids.
exactly.
now...

she takes in a deep breath
and pulls out her clipboard.

our question is going to be:
        what do you like to do that keeps you stress-free?

306

de-BORE-uh is in her room
and the rap music is playing in the hall
and she says to me as i walk by HAAAY GURL
and i look in at her and smile at her arms swinging above her nappy head
she motions for me to come in

i come in and she says HAAY DANCE WIFF ME
and i say nooo not me.
and she says i saw you in the hall the other day.
i saw you dance.

i start to dance.
i start shaking my head all around
and my hair is flying and hitting my face
and my limp white arms
are doing things they've never done before
all to the beat of this muthafuckin song
and we just dance together for a little while
and she stops and watches me and i DANCE, baby.
i DANCE.

she starts laughing
she starts laughing to where she folds over in half
and her hands are on her knees she is bending over
and her eyes are squinty and smiley
because she is laughing at my dance
and she starts to cry tears down her face
oh gurl oh gurl you crazy muthafucka
and i start laughing too
cracking into hysterics
crazy-person hysterics while i DANCE, baby.
i DANCE
and she cracks up has to sit down on her bed
and rests and wipes tears from her eyes.

oh Looord.
oh LORD!
lord.
you crazy muthafucka.
you craaaay-zee *bitch*!

and i say i like you.
and she says i like you too.
you's funny.
you're funny too, de-BORE-uh.
thanks.

and i walk out of the room
my teeth just keep on showing.

307

visitation is from one to four on saturday, sunday and major holidays.

my parents come at one and stay with me until four.
i highly appreciate it.
i don't think i've ever enjoyed spending time
with my parents more than from one to four on saturdays and sundays
and major holidays.

today
they come with a big bag **full of books**.
mom says these are from Kelsey.
and these are from me.
she hands me three fashion magazines.

one is a *vogue*.

ohmygod mom. ohgod THANK you.
i start flipping through it immediately and mom puts her hand down on the front cover
easing it shut.

don't you want to save it for later?

oh.

right.

i suppose i should.

i shut it and sit upright with my hands in my lap.
the way i suppose i should.

i look through the books. ohmygod. oh lord. so many kurt vonnegut novels, oooh and a
j.d. salinger short stories collection! i can't wait to start reading them all at once.

inside vonnegut's *hocus pocus* i see a letter from kelsey and an envelope that says my
            name on it.
i want to read them now i want to read them now but i wait.

because
i suppose i should.

after mom and dad bring **the books and the magazines**
i feel a little like myself again
and i invest my whole being into them.

i pour over them
i breathe them in
i may have even licked a couple of the pages.

this was serious.
this was *vogue*.
this was vonnegut.
this was heaven.

i read and i read and i read
and miss amy tells me
you better not let any of those
girls get a hold of those
because
(she looks around slyly)
they'll STEAL 'em!

and so i write my name in
them all
and i keep them by my side.

but when jackie asks if she can look at
my *people*, i couldn't deny her the happiness
of a juicy read, now, could i?

i hand it to her, but say
these are all i got
so sit right here.

she silently nods
and starts flipping
through the pages furiously.

that's when i remember.
kelsey's letter!

inside the front cover
of kurt vonnegut's ingenious novel
hocus pocus
i can see the corner
of a little piece of looseleaf.

i pull it out and my bones
are shaking.

it is her handwriting.
it is really her's.

i read it and my eyes tear up
and my lips struggle to smile
which ends up looking very gruesome.

jackie looks up from my *people* magazine and says
what's wrong?
then looks at the scrawl of handwriting across
the notebook paper.
what's that?
she grabs at it
and i jerk away and my sad sick little smile
turns to an angry pout.
what the hell are you doing?

i just wanted to read it.

it's mine.

sorry.

it's okay.
it's just it's... it's just that it's mine.
sorry.

okay.
it's all good.

okay.

phew.

yeah.
really.
phew.

she hands me back my magazine.
we look at each other awkwardly
and our eyes shift all around
and i get up and walk away
and she just goes over to play
cards with bradley.

how weird was that?

we get in the horseshoe for miss amy's group therapy.

"the horseshoe" is a semicircle of crazy young people
sitting in generic plastic blue desks
biting their fingernails and staring emptily out of bloodred eyeballs.

as i am moving my desk to create the semicircle, i catch a glimpse of morgan the crazy patient
hunched over with her back facing all of us.
i stretch my neck out to look at what she's doing,
and i immediately wish i hadn't.

i suck in a mouthful of saliva and the blood in my veins stops flowing for a second.

she is *digging* into herself.
she has her arm outstretched flat onto her lap
and she is DIGGING (oh poor morgan what are you **digging for** what are you trying to *find?*)
her short jagged fingernails into the pasty flesh of her arm and her vein is popping open
            and the blood
oh God the blood is dripping down to her wrist.

i jerk my head away.
what should i *do*??
i ignore it.

miss amy dips the flesh of her silken fingertips into an attractive little tub of lotion.

kids, this is my magic stuff. my secret.

she stands up and comes right up to me.

she smiles a beautiful smile.

try some.

i try to smile back
and i dip my own dirty leathery fingertips into her magic lotion
and spread it all over my hands.

i look up at her face.

wow.
it's wonderful.

(but morgan is bleeding *every*where.)

there is one group therapy that big D does not attend

we are solemnly informed that her grandfather has passed away

and we pretend to care with sad eyes that are full of false promise and phony remorse.

after group i go back into my room
and big d is sitting on her bed silently
looking down at her humongous feet.

she polishes her size twelve sneakers every day with a very heavy grease.
she opens the drawer of her desk and pulls out her hygiene kit.
she looks over at me, every morning, and whispers
you better not tell anybody i have this in here. it's contraband.
every morning i say
i won't tell. don't worry darlene.

but now she is not polishing.
she is not whispering.
she is not even humming obnoxiously.
her jigsaw puzzle still lies on her desk,
unfinished and abandoned.

are you okay darlene?

no.

were you very close to him?

yes.

i'm so sorry.

it's okay.

is there something i can do?

no.

okay.

thanks.

you're welcome.

g'night.

goodnight, darlene. sweet dreams.

during breakfast jen sits beside me
and de-BORE-uh on the other side
and across from me, the satan worshipper.

we eat cereal and milk from little **pre-packaged** cartons.

jen says
chelsea there was this fuckin big ass spider in my fuckin room last night.

i say
oh.

she says
i tried to fuckin kill it but it ran out.

i say
oh.

she says
i think it's in you and fuckin big D's room now.

i say
oh.

she says
she's fuckin *fat*.

i still sneak pencils into my room
so i can write at night
i am a **pencil sneak**

jen told me yesterday
that she has about twenty hidden under her mattress
not that i believed her.

and big D can't tell on me
because i know about her hygiene box.

so it is all good.
i write and i draw
and nobody says nothin.

if you are on level three you get to go to **movie night** on friday.

i can't go even though i'm on level three.
because you also have to have been here for a full week.

i'm kind of sad that i can't go to movie night just because
i haven't been crazy as long as the rest of them have.

when i tell my daddy about it on the phone during calls at night
he says "a full week? then i hope you never get to go to movie night."

at lunch i am standing in line with the mob
de-BOR-uh and jen, meowing girl and nasty-ass rhonda.

everyone is talking about movie night.
i say shut up you guys and de-BORE-uh says yuh, muthafuckas. i cain't go neither.

so they change the subject.
at the freezer, de-BORE-uh tells me to get an eskimo pie.
every day she tells me which ice cream bar to choose.
i always listen to her
because though she is probably my best friend here
i am still scared to death of her.

as we pass the table of little kids from "child unit one"
a little black girl with a pretty weave looks up at de-BORE-uh
then starts laughing at her little friends after she walks by.

de-BORE-uh sits down beside me with a very angry look
on her face.

what's wrong, toneisha?

that muthafuckin **little ho**.

who?

that lil ho ovah thurr.

i look to where she points and i see a little black girl staring back
then turning to her friends and whispering, occasionally pointing to de-BORE-uh.

de-BORE-uh stands up when the little girl points and she yells across the cafeteria
YOU NAPPY ASS MUTHAFUCKIN BITCH! YOU MUTHAFUCKIN *NEVAH* POINT AT ME WITH YO
MUTHAFUCKIN FILTHY-ASS FINGERS! YOU FUCKIN *WAINCH*! YOU LIL *HO*!

and she starts to walk toward the little girl who is shaking in her chair with big white
eyes popping from their sockets, de-BORE-uh's hands are outstretched and her fingers
are flexing in and out, in and out...

when a nurse comes up from behind and grabs de-BORE-uh, puts her in a hold and the
whole cafeteria goes silent except for gasps and occasional snickers from the adolescent
boys unit's table.

de-BORE-uh cries out NOOOO NOO DON'T YOU MUTHAFUCKIN PUT YO HANDS ON ME! GET
YO MUTHAFUCKIN HANDS OFFA ME! YOU MUTHAFUCKIN BITCH GET YOU MUTHAFUCKIN
HANDS THE FUCK OFFA ME! but the nurse keeps her in a tight hold and terrance runs up
and helps her drag de-BORE-uh out of the cafeteria as she yells IF YOU GIVE ME ANOTHA
ONE UH THOSE MUTHA*FUCKIN* SHOTS...

after she is gone
everything is back to normal
and i bite into my eskimo pie.

i think inside my crazy little brain,
i hope they don't give poor de-BORE-uh any of those motherfucking shots.

de-BORE-uh gets in some other fight

after the tranquilizers wear off

and she yells yells yells

down the white sterile hallway

so long long long

such a drawn-out hallway

gets smaller and smaller

seems *miles* long

that hallway

oh

she yells yells yells:

i'm goin tah muthafuckin REHAB
in TWO fuckin days fuh christ's sake
so why should i give a *shit* what you fuckas think?

bradley and i are playing cards again
and his leg's touching mine beneath the
desk
and i'm ignoring it.

all the sudden he stops dealing cards out
and stares
at me
hard.

he flips over a card
and it is a king.

he says
"it's **the suicidal king**.
see?"
he points
"he has a knife in his head
...get it?"

and then
bradley gets up and
walks away
and i am all alone with
my thoughts.

i hate that feeling
when i step out of that cold shower and get dressed
in nasty worn out clothes
and my hair is wet and my makeup is gone
and i have to walk into the day room
exposed to all of these people.

i hate it when i am **still wet** and bradley
asks me to play a game of cards.

my hair is dripping on the desk.

did you have a nice shower?
he smiles.

no.
i say.

oh. i'm sorry.
he shuffles.
why not?

it was cold.
i sigh and avoid his pink eyes.

you know you look like velma from *scooby doo*?
what?
i said you look just like velma from *scooby doo*.
oh.

he shuffles the cards again.

jackie gets out of the shower
and sees us playing cards.

can i play?
she says.

she is holding a stack of photographs.

you know what, i don't wanna play, really.
you can play with him.
can i look at your pictures?

okay.
she hands them to me and
rushes over to take my spot
across from bradley.

> the pictures show her with long curly hair
> that is now spiky and short.
> she is with a horse.

do you ride?

oh yes.

that must be fantastic.
i love horses.

i have three.

wow.

i look at more pictures.

is this your dad?

yes.
he's dead.

i'm sorry.

yeah.

the next picture is a dog
the next is a cat
the next is another picture of her
and in her eyes i can see something different in jackie

something... *alive.*

during group with murray
i am sitting by de-BOR-uh
and somehow she
gets us waaaay off topic
and we end up talking about **george dubya** again
and how he is the anti-Christ
and about the ridiculous rise in gas prices and
de-BORE-uh says
and what's with muthafuckin cigarettes?
they costin like five fuckin dollas now.
i like those!
i don't have five mothafuckin dollas urrytime
i wanna muthafuckin cigarette.

and murray just laughs.

because de-BORE-uh's neck has
no bones
it wiggles around
and jerks and snaps
while she talks.

so much attitude
in such a little short stubby
package.

during visitation
with mom and dad
i say
can you please put kelsey on **my call list?**

and mom says
sure sweetie.
we'll do that today.

bradley tells me over a
very creepy game of cards
that he is going to jail.

i don't say
WHAT FOR?

i don't want to know.

so
i say

really?

and he says

yeah.

and i say

i don't really feel like playing cards anymore.

meowing girl is sitting all alone
and her curly wet hair is dripping
cause she just got out of the shower
and she is drawing with a pencil
so all the staff is watching her very closely

i change desks and sit by her,
interested.

what are you drawing?

oh
a comic.

can i see?

sure.

wow. you're really good.

thanks.
the main character... well. she's really interesting cause she's half cat. see, she has a
kitty tail. and look at her ears!

ha. that's cool.

mister jim yells
chelsea!

and i walk over to him.

he says
phone call?

and i brace myself.
and i think of her face.
and i say

yes, please.

i sit in the chair.

the phone-calling chair.

he says
who you callin?

i say
her name is kelsey.

he says
okay.
you pick it up when it rings.

he dials on his phone.

the phone beside me rings.

it hurts my ears
but i pick it up.

i hear him say
the name of the hospital
and i am so ashamed.

i hear him say
would you like to speak with chelsea?

i hear her say yes.

i watch him hang up.

i say

hi.

HI!

and i sigh.

i sigh relief.

and she sighs.

she sighs relief.

and we remember each other's voices
and for a little while

we remember each other's eyes.

but we hear each other's sighs

and we both heard mister jim
say the name of the hospital

and we both knew my plan.

and we both knew it all.

so somehow it is not the same.

kelsey said	i said
it's so good to hear your voice	i know
i miss you	i miss you too
i love you	i love you too

(this is when we start to cry but we don't let the tears make any sounds)

kelsey said	i said
how are you?	it's so weird here.
yeah.	you know that book *one flew over the cuckoo's nest*?
yeah.	it's just like that.
oh.	it's so crazy.
oh. when are you coming back?	i don't know.
i miss you a lot.	yeah.
i wanted to-	i have to go.
oh.	it's been five minutes.
okay.	i'm only allowed to talk for five minutes.
i love you.	i love you too.
so much.	sooo much.
bye.	bye.

i hand the phone to mister jim
who is waiting

and i ask miss amy if i
can go to sleep early tonight.

she says
sure, baby.

so i tuck myself into **my sheets**
that are not even close to white anymore
covered in my salt
and my dirt
and my horror.

my pillow is covered in my tears
and my makeup
and my hair
and my slobber
and the parts of my mind
that leak out while i sleep.

same shit, different day

i wake up at 7AM

and it is breakfast time.

i just have some cereal like always.

then we're back from the caff and we have goals group.

then we have free time in the day room.

then we have FUCKING school.

then we have group therapy.

then we go to lunch and i have something nasty like always.

then we have group therapy.

then we have free time in the day room.

then we have dinner in the caff and i have something nasty like always.

then we have goals group.

then we have group therapy.

then we have free time in the day room.

then we have showers.

then we have phone calls.

then we go to sleep and i never really sleep a wink like always.

at lunch time
in the caff
little nicky starts telling me all about her
crazy life and she twists her frizzy curly blonde hair
around her pinkie finger and smiles as she tells me
like it is such a silly story.
such a silly life.

but here is what she actually says:

-both of her parents died in a car crash while they were on drugs

but as she tells me she laughs and she smiles and
she twists her frizzy curly blonde hair around her pinkie finger.

another group therapy with miss amy:
(because these are the only ones i really remember)

we are in the group dungeon.
i am all huddled up with de-BORE-uh because
it is muthafuckin cold
in this hellhole, says she.

miss amy looks ravishing
and there is something artful, something so
imprecisely abstract about her beauty
that she just radiates unequaled brilliance.
matchless grandeur.

i love her.

i start to actually believe that **she is my mother.**

she says babies.
we are gonna talk about constructive criticism.
that's when we all zone out.
psychoanalytical mumbo-jumbo bores
us out of our *minds* at this point in our personal journeys
to curing our out-of-control mental illnesses.
so she starts at one side of the room
and something magical happens.

she starts with:

bradley.
she says.
honey, you are so nice to all the other kids. you have this luster about you and you are a generous and caring person. i think your biggest problem is simply that you are trying to hide this sweet boy from the rest of the world by putting up a tough front.

bradley blushes and says
that ain't true.
i AM tough.
and he frowns.

miss amy smiles.

toneisha.
(that's what they call de-BORE-uh since the *incident*)
you are full of spunk, attitude, personality, and you are highly opinionated.
(everyone smiles to themselves: that's one way to put it.)
these qualities, if you use them correctly, can get you far in life. you can pretty much do whatever it is you want to do, as long as you can learn to control that temper and you can stay off the drugs.

de-BORE-uh smiles and says thank yah miss amy.

chelsea.
(i freeze)
i haven't known you very long but you have something in you. there's a certain something in you that nobody else has. it's something different. something unique. because even though most of the time you spend in the day room or around other kids, you are quiet and to yourself, still you don't seem distant or shy. when kids come up to you to talk you generously accept them. you give everyone a chance. and you are a very smart girl.
(i wince. a very smart girl.)
you just need to work hard on opening up and showing us all that special something you got inside.

thank you, miss amy.

jen.
(jen is looking at the wall and munching her nails)
you are probably the strongest person i have ever met in my life. not only strong physically, because we ALL know you can beat up a girl like THAT, (we all laugh), but also strong mentally, and strong emotionally. you can get through so many things and not even be fazed by it. and your leg, jen. a week ago i watched you guys playin kickball outside. jen, you ran faster and harder than all the other kids. you were the star. and i'm sure lotsa these kids don't even know about your prosthetic.
(my mouth drops open. i can' t help it. miss amy notices and smiles at me.)
you didn't know, chelsea?
(i shake my head.)
see, hon, chelsea didn't even know!
you are a great girl, jen, and you just need to work on displaying that to everyone.

thanks, amy.

she goes on and on like this and her words about me keep circling around in my brain and i hear the words about the others as she continues and all of the courtesy about the room is just too much of a good thing for me and i start to cry a lot very suddenly, but nobody says anything.

whenever they ask me
WHERE IS YOUR SPECIAL PLACE
i close my eyes
and i think of
kerrville, texas
and the guadalupe river

in kerrville

i walk
       alone

                   completely alone

hearing the slapping of my
shoes on the gravel road
and i take turns without
knowing it because the map
is engraved into my mind
and i

                   stop.

because i am walking too fast.

so
i
slow
down
and
look
up
into
the
black
sky
and
this
is
the
only
place
that
i've
ever
been
able
to
see
every   single   star.

and i breathe out in a
hazy exhausted impressed
sort of way and i get to
the place and slip between
two bushes and feel as if
the night is wrapped around
me and all is so utterly black
that it is suffocating
me in a loving, sweet,
noxious sweetness and
i dip my toes into the
blackness that is the
guadalupe river and the
water looks like cool
black syrup but feels more
like the way lemon iced tea
feels on the back of a july throat
and i slip into the syrup yes i slip
into the tea and it
swallows me up and i swim
around and create little ebony circles
all around me and it is

                            silent.

how can you spend a week with a person and not
have any idea that they have a fake leg?

how can you spend a week eating nothing but ice cream
sandwiches and pasteurized cheese?

how can you spend a week with no sleep,
a week with no art,
a week with no kelsey,
a week with no wayne?

how can you spend a week
with no feelings

a week with no brain

a week with no sunshine

a week with no rain?

how can you spend a week
imagining catching a train
and riding away
forever.

oh God.

is this now my home

is this the only way
i can live
without feeling alone

is this where
i

(gasp)

belong?

can you hear me, God?
did you catch that last part?

school time

and i do some work
wondering what i'm worth
watching the clock
tick and tock

what am i worth?

and i scratch my name into the desk
and there's a knock on the door
and something in my throat
is jiggling.

it is murray.

chelsea.

he says.

his voice so deep and relaxing.

come on.

time to see murray

and he says

you know

(it seems so long until the words come out)

you might be able to leave tomorrow.

something inside cracks
and something inside shivers

i want to leave and
i want to stay forever.

i want to hold the 7
all tight in my arms

i wanna blow bubbles
i wanna live on a farm.

i want anything
everything
but i still feel alarm

can anyone keep me from self bodily harm?

i keep talking to murray though

as if i am SO READY
so ready
i'm all better
everything is back to fantastic
i promise you i swear
PLEASE I'M BEGGING YOU TO FUCKING BELIEVE ME
I'M ON MY KNEES HERE

and he gets the point so
i go to sleep that night
smiling a little

biting my finger
until it breaks the skin
and i remember that i am ALIVE.

i have blood within.

a living soul.

a living sin.

i am ALIVE.

oh no.
oh no.

i'm alive.

oh no.

thank you.

let me live.
let me leave.
let me live.

the next morning

we go through the routine
and breakfast tastes
extra stale this morning,
don't it de-BORE-uh?

yuh.

when i hear "yeah"
from *usher*'s mouth in the morning
it is the last straw
and i kick my bed
violently
over and over and over
and i throw my sheets and
my pillow
on the ground
and i yell
I HATE THIS FUCKING SONG
I FUCKING HAAATE THIS FUCKING SONG

and big D
is sitting on her bed covering her mouth
and her eyes are widened.

jen is in the hallway
and she just smiles.

he takes me to his office.

how do you feel about leaving?

am i leaving?

yes. you are leaving.

i'm leaving?

yes.

oh.

don't you want to leave.

yes. please.

alright.

let's go talk to your parents. okay?

(sigh) alright.

there they are again.

this time more scared.

this time more stern.

eyes more aware.

murray is different.

everything is heavy.

everything smells thick.

nobody blinks.

we talk for a while

and i don't remember much

about it just PLEASE LET ME

THE FUCK OUT OF THIS PLACE

and the look on murray's face

very serious when he talks about

my drinking and my mary jane

and i nod slowly, i know, i know.

JUST PLEASE

kind sir

PLEASE

LET ME THE FUCK OUT OF THIS PLACE!!

there are forms to sign
but it goes by so quick
and soon there i am
back in my room
gathering my things
can you believe it?

little nicky with her
car crash parents
is sitting in front of
the teevee and she says
are you leaving chelsea?

and i say yes.
a little sadly,
a part of me notices.
i want to take her with me.
i see bradley's eyes and
the envy in jen's tense
forehead and i want to take
them all with me what will
happen to them when i leave?

i gather my poetry and my clothes
and my magazines
and my books and my hygiene kit
and then a nurse goes and gets the rest
of my clothes from contraband and sharps.

and **i feel so artificial.**

looking around,
i wasn't here long.
only my whole life.
i didn't learn much.
only everything there is to know.
i didn't cry too many tears.
only five billion.
i didn't age too many years.
only three trillion.

TIME TO LEAVE!

have all your stuff?

YES LET ME OUT!

and mom and dad are there with me
and little brother benjamin
hugs me tight
and i think

tonight
TONIGHT
i'll sleep in my bed
and all that black
will be out of my head.

oh gosh.
YEAH.

and they put their arms around me
and murray shakes my hand
and i say goodbye to miss amy
and de-BORE-uh toneisha
secretly hoping to see them again.

and i walk through the blue door
behind it is freedom

what will the real world
feel like on my skin?

it's opening.

it's opening...

it's open...

i am out.

there are cars.

there are trees.

there are birds.

there are bees.

there is wind.

there are buildings.

there are clouds.

there is sky.

i do not wonder why.

but my eyes start to cry -

and what the fuck is THAT?

mom and i
STOP.

and benjamin and dad walk on
through the parking lot
hurrying to get in the car.
hurrying to normal.
make it all normal again.

but mom and i see
on the ground.

there it is.

what the fuck
no way.

what the fuck.
no WAY.

and i'm not even lying
true story
TRUE story.

what the fuck was there lying
on the ground
right outside
of that mental ward
where i died?

it was
a

rubik's cube.

and all the sudden
i stop in my tracks

lean over
and i think i'm having a heart attack
oh lookee
would you look at THAT?

i lean over
and i think i'm having a heart attack.

i pick it up
this perfect specimen.

am i crazy?

am i crazy?

am i crazy?

am i crazy?

no.
because right here in my hand
in the palm of my hand
is a little miracle
a little rubik's cube
and lemme tell you something

it is **SOLVED**.

i carry it **in my hands**
crying tears down my face
and my mom and i embrace

she keeps saying
"weird, huh?"
wanting to say something
about the Big Man Upstairs
but i'm glad she doesn't
because i already know
i already caught that part
i don't need her help.

but i do need her help
getting to the car.
opening the door.
seatbelt.
wipe those tears.
i open my hand
and there it is, inside.

a *rubik's cube*.

i laugh out loud.

good one, God.

i gotta hand it to you, Big Guy.

you got me there.

we drove away from THAT PLACE
and i held the rubik's cube in my hands
i rolled it around on my palm and i fingered
the little colored squares
i caressed the perfection.

dad said **how about chinese?**
and i said delicious.
i'm sick of fucking fake cheese on a bun.

he drives the whole family to a chinese buffet and i don't notice how out-of-sync i
am with the world until i see my reflection in the glass door of the restaurant.

i still have loony hair.
there are greasy spots all over my wrinkled clothes.
i am wearing slippers
and my pants do not have a drawstring.
i have on absolutely no makeup
and my eyes are still red.
perma-red from overcrying.
my nails are violently bitten down
and the blackbluegreen
circles under my eyes are foreboding.

i try hard to ignore the reflection
but it is a very scary picture
and i am immediately self-conscious about
the people looking at me, the people eating
chinese food in their greasy vinyl booths.

they don't even know how lucky they are.

i get some food and the rubik's cube is still
stuck in my head. i left it in the car because i don't
have a purse or pockets.
i left it in the car because it is too distracting.
but i can't stop thinking about it anyway.

how very strange.
i don't talk the whole meal
and neither do my parents.

i am finally free.
and now there is nothing to say.

after i eat a plateful i am done.
my little compacted stomach is filled
and it took me as long to eat my one plate as
it took my parents to eat three.

at the end
dad reaches for the tab
and i absentmindedly reach for a
fortune cookie.

still thinking about the rubik's cube.
still thinking about de-BOR-uh toneisha.
still thinking about how great it will be to shave my legs once i get home.

i break open the yellow shell
and inside
it says:

We would often be sorry if our
wishes came true.

Epilogue

Epilogue

dear mom and dad,

i have something that i have been waiting to tell you. i don't want you to start worrying. stop worrying right now. it is an exciting thing. i'm very excited. i just haven't told you because i am nervous that you won't be nearly as excited as i am, and that would probably break my heart.

i have been letting people read my book. just friends and stuff. and as you both know, it is really coming along. it's about three hundred something pages now. i think that's exciting. i let kelsey take it home and since i have talked to her dad about all of this, i thought it would be neat if he read it, since he showed interest when i told him about it. kelsey *did* let him read it, and she also let her mom. they loved it. they called me once they finished it and they each talked to me for about fifteen minutes about how much they liked it. they both said "i couldn't put it down!" that's what everyone says. but then her dad told me about his book. i don't know if i told you guys, but he's writing a book for some company, and it's become a really big deal at their house. he got paid for it in advance and he has a publishing contract even though he hasn't finished yet. but another part of the deal is that he gets to be co-president of this publishing company, if he wants, with this other guy. he said yes. after he read my book he told me about all of this, and he said that he talked to the other president, and told him how great my book was. the guy said, "so let's publish it!" we don't know anything for sure, but he has sent him parts of it, and it's starting to get serious. of course, they can't do anything without my consent, or your consent. and i haven't told them to do anything with it yet. i just wanted to wait until i was sure before i made it into some great big thing. he even told me that i could get paid beforehand.
well... you *said* you wanted me to get a job!

just kidding.

i know that in the past this book has hurt you both, and scared you both, and made you both angry, and made you both sad. so your initial reaction is probably that you don't want anything so personal published. i am aware that it is personal, and that this is our family's business. i am aware that it is very heavy, and there are some things that everybody doesn't need to know about.

last night, when charlie called in the middle of the night, he called to tell me that he had let his friend Betty read my book and that he invited her over to talk about it. she was holding it in her hands, and right when she opened her mouth to talk about it, she started to cry. she said it affected her so much because she identified with all of my emotions exactly. with my frustration, with my depression, with my anger, and even with my happiness. she told charlie that she had been to an institution twice for the same thing i went in for, and it completely changed her life. and for a long time she's been trying to get over it, trying to push it out of the way. but reading my book helped her remember what it was like, and in a way it kind of released all of the tension that has been attached to that topic for so long. it cleansed her mind, and it made her feel much better knowing that she was not all alone. she said she cried the whole time she read it.

learning that it can affect one person like that makes me want to share it with everyone.

another example: my friend amy who was wanting to commit suicide read my book. and she also enjoyed it a lot. she had been cutting herself and after she read my book, she went and told her dad about it and now they are in counseling.

can you believe that?

but when i think back, the only reason i agreed to go to therapy with gina jordan was because i had read a book called "prozac nation". in this memoir, the author elizabeth wurtzel gets very depressed and starts dragging down her family and her friends with her extreme unhappiness. she accepts her personality as permanently malcontent and starts to live her life negatively. absolutely believing that she will never get better. which was what i had started to do. i had started to thrive in my depression, believing that it was just a part of who i am. but later on in the book, things start getting worse and worse. she starts experimenting with drugs and sex and she ends up hurting everyone around her and destroying herself completely. i cried the whole time i read it. because there where these segments that were just her describing her emotions. and my emotions were identical. i started underlining all the sentences that i identified with. and soon i was underlining whole pages at a time. that's when i started thinking, man. this is just how she started. look what happened to her. do i want to be that? so i gave myself up and i made a commitment to get better.

i believe that things like this can and will help other people that are in need.

i believe that my book can touch people's lives.

i believe that i can make a difference with this.

something that i have invested so much time in finally has a purpose.

another thing you might worry about is yourselves. you don't want everyone to think that you are bad parents. but believe it or not, you are NOT portrayed negatively in my book. i mean, there are parts, of course, where i am angry with you, or we get in a fight, but everyone does that to their parents. everyone goes through that. i never once in the entire book blamed anything on you or said that i hate you. because i love you both and i truly believe that you are the sole reason that i am still here today.

i have decided, also, that if this even happens, i will be working under a different name. all the names in the book will be changed also. this way, the book will not be an exposé, but a story. a story that can help people, not a diary or a journal for people that know me to indulge in to get all the details of my life.

i am of course going to let you read it. i am almost finished. but this time when you read it, i want you to think of it as a story written by a girl who WAS hurting. not a existing cry for help from your own daughter. all the things in this book are from the past, and have been lived out and completed. just because i have been *writing* them lately, does not mean i have been *feeling* them lately. it actually means that i am now comfortable enough with what happened to let it all out and get past it. this is not only for others to benefit from, but also for me to let out everything that i have experienced. it is a tool that has helped me come to terms with my emotions and my problems. i think that this is really a positive thing and that the way it has turned out is quite a miracle.

imagine me, a sixteen-year-old published author.

can you?

can you *imagine* it?

how amazing would that be?

i just hope SO MUCH that you can see this from my point of view, and be excited. because i have spent several sleepless weeks trying very hard to see it from yours. trying to come up with ways that it will make us all happy. i talked to murray about it today and he said that he thinks it is the most wonderful idea. he says that he would buy tons of copies and give them to his patients and ask them to circle the feelings that they can relate to. he would use it as a therapeutic tool. MY book, a therapeutic tool. a way to heal people that have the same problems that i have had. it was his idea for me to write you this letter. he said this way you would have time to think about it before you spoke. and i would have time to tell you what i think without any interruptions. He says that when someone has this much to say on a subject and prepares a conversation, it never ends up that they get it all said.

i'm pretty sure i've said all i needed to say now.

i don't want you to be upset about this.

i want you to understand first WHY i want it published:
- to help other people
- to express myself
- to get some closure on the subject

and i want you to think about it for a little while, then we can talk it over and you can tell me what you think. thank you for reading all of this. i'm sorry i've kept it from you so long, but i've just been very nervous about it.

       love,

          chelsea